Enabled

Ceci and Lucy Sturman

Enabled is dedicated to our parents,
John and Elizabeth, without whom none
of this would be possible. Your
devotion, your kindness, your love.
Thank you.

Contents

There are many things
I am
and what I do best at.
I'm not giving up or stopping myself from
everything in life-
I can be a challenge at times and get into messes
all along the way
but I try to be strong and move past them.
I may not be perfect and that's okay.
I do wish I was normal
without a learning challenge,
being like my friends for once
doing fun stuff
independently.
But, if I was normal,
there won't be a Lucy
and without a Lucy, a world would not be there
for her.

In the summers when you were young, you would
pass by a store that made saltwater taffy, you
would stop and stare through the window at the
heavy rolls of it, blue and pink and, your
favorite, emerald green.

You would watch the rolls slowly twist and turn
into themselves:
           form themselves, and then destroy
           themselves, and then form themselves
           again.
It brought you a sweet sadness and

     now that you have grown to despise the way
it sticks to your teeth, you will still upon
occasion remember how it formed
    and wonder, if
slowly,
    you have begun to form yourself again.

Formation

I didn't exist for three years.
Well, two years and ten months exactly.

When I feel worst it is when she is not there,
and when she was not there for two years and ten
months my mind decided that it was so bored with
me that it hated me actually; not only that, it
began to stage a multi-phased attack.

The warmth of my parents was almost enough but
because of language barriers they were not
equipped to dig up the seeds - planted just deep
enough to disrupt the patience of my mind in the
early development stages.

It was patient, my mind,

all it did was plant its seeds

and wait, and wait.

But when she came it stopped for a while,

it was disarmed with the feeling of being known
and of loving something so much it does not
matter whether you love yourself or not

and for years and years, it couldn't catch a
break
feeding off of minor insecurities and girls that
chirped and boys that ignored and turbulent plane
rides

but she loved me enough for the both of us

then
little by little,
it started to feed
more and more

until

    WAKE UP

    SHE IS GOING AWAY

    SHE IS GOING AWAY WITHOUT THE OTHER ONE

    IT IS TIME, MEN,
    IT IS TIME TO ATTACK

when I went away, when we were apart for the
first time in 15 years,
they took us both down.

      We cannot exist apart, my sister and I:
            we must exist as one.
        It is the only way we can exist.

My sister

As sisters
There is love everywhere
It's in the air
The hearts belonging to the sisters
Shows beautiful love
And you know by the heart
They're best friends
Sharing heartwarming memories
Catching from falling
Most of the time hugging
And conversations
Supporting each other
Every time and everywhere
Sisters together
Hold hands
For protection
I love you
Just from the heart
They stand strong together
Making promises
Keeping secrets
Connecting by heart
As the love shows
They have each other
Laughing at anything
"Sisters by chance
Friends by choice"
I love you sister
I love you too sister
I want you to know
By giving you a blessing
You're in my heart
You're in my heart too

We made it

She told me,

We made it.

I never hear more aggressive words come out of my
sister's mouth than when she is comforting me.
When she is demanding that I know of my worth, of
her love for me, when she is fighting my demons
for me.
She knows, somehow, more than anyone else in my
life, that when I am feeling my worst, what I
need is to hear boldness and confidence and to
trust in words to shatter my own doubt.

I called my sister tonight as I was walking back
from the gym and I told her that I was struggling
with my anxiety and sadness that I didn't feel
like I was good enough, that I couldn't do it on
my own.

She told me

Ceci,
You are so intelligent. You are so, so smart. And
so many people love you. So many people care
about you. You have such a big support system.

She told me,

Ceci,
I am here for you. When we are not together I am
in your heart and you are in mine. We are
connected to each other. God gave us each other
and I know that we fight sometimes but
WE MADE IT

She told me that she missed me and she loves me
so much and she wished that we could go to our
favorite restaurant - Sisters Thai - together. I
told her to come to live with me in New York,
very seriously. She said she had to check her
schedule, which was fair.

When I told her I was going to hang up she said,
                    wait Ceci - one more thing.
Yes?
  Pray to God. Pray to him. He is right there next
to you, he is holding you, he loves you. You are
                    not alone. Just pray.

My eyes welled. So much that I had to stop
walking.

Wow, Lucy. You're right. Your words are so
powerful.

                    I'm not as good as mom
she says.

No seriously, I told her, you heal me. You help
me so much.

                    Aw Ceci, I'm blushing.

I know I am your big sister and I am supposed to
support you, but you have supported me so much
you have no idea.

                    Ceci, you always support me.

A sister is a special thing to have and a special thing to be. According to science, if we have sisters, we're supposed to be kinder, better communicators, to feel safer and more loved. Naturally, not all of us will have the same organic relationship with our sisters, not everyone will feel that warmth chemically correlated to femininity and sisterhood. Every relationship, sibling or elsewise, is different than the next.

And mine is different. Awesome in the most mystical sense of the term and in ways science can and cannot explain. We are not more different than others, not less different. Just different enough to write a book about.

As my sister and I are just beginning to understand how our hearts are intertwined, just beginning to understand that there is no logical rhythm to our worlds and our words, only an emotional.

Down Syndrome

I was born
With a disability
Called Down Syndrome
I was young
So I didn't know
I had it.
I think I felt nothing was
Wrong about me.

People must have
Thought "What's wrong with her?"
I thought to myself I was normal

As I have grown slowly
It has given a life change
For me
I guess that was a thought
From my mind.
It affected
Me to find out
All of my thoughts
Turned into questions
So quickly
I guess I felt uncomfortable
About it
As it sank into me
While I was growing
I began to think
What is DS?
As I was thinking
About my questions
I felt so uncomfortable
In my own skin
I felt like a monster inside of me
And on the outside
I was afraid
Of what people
Would think of me
I also had a thought
Would people
Like me

Enabled

I felt like
No one would want me
Or like me
I guess the feeling
Of being an outcast
Became the biggest concern
For me to deal with.

Growth

What I remember first about my little sister is her crying. Constantly, all the time. I remember how deep her cries came through her throat and I remember that I didn't like the sound of them, but to be fair I don't think she liked me much either.

My mom told me that, once, she picked Lucy up from her crib and put her in my toddler bed. They did that whenever Lucy wasn't crying — forced sister bonding. And sometimes it worked, but this time, Lucy stared at me for a while and then she turned her little self around so she wasn't facing me and sobbed her eyes out to the wall. She didn't stop until my mom put her back in her crib.

I remember the night when I realized just how different my sister was. I was almost four.

Dad read to me every night and one night he walked in and said that we would be starting a new book. The book was called *We'll Paint The Octopus Red*. After he got about three pages in, I stopped listening because I realized that in the pictures, the 'sister' looked a lot like Lucy and not like me or my parents or other people I knew. I was confused. Does Lucy know her? Dad picked up on it.

Lucy looks like this girl, doesn't she?
Yes!

Cec, your sister is special. She is different from you and me, but that's okay. She was born with Down Syndrome, and we love her so much.

When I was three years old, Down Syndrome didn't make sense to me. I thought that everyone's sister was like Lucy. I thought that everyone's sister never stopped crying and screaming. I thought that everyone's sister was always in the doctor's office and that everyone's family was always in the waiting room. I thought that everyone's mom cried in her bedroom every night. When my dad told me that my sister was born with Down Syndrome, I didn't understand why I wasn't born with Down Syndrome. And I still don't.

Having Down Syndrome

There are challenges that I have to face.

I have a hard time
remembering most stuff,
I think people won't like me on the spot at a
job,
I can't look at the board and paper at the same
time
and I lose my place,
following complicated directions,
answering "why" questions are difficult,
people staring at me in public,
I don't like repeating myself
If people don't understand me,

I HATE, HATE, HATE, REPEATING MYSELF.

I overcome anything that's not easy for me to do
and face the fears that I have.
I can be a challenge at times and get into messes
all along the way,
But I always try to be strong and move past them.

But, if I was normal there won't be a Lucy
And without a Lucy, a world would not be there
for her.

What I remember next varies. Some memories I'll never be able to erase; I'm predestined to play them on a reel, or to select one out of the bunch at the appropriate trigger. Others are hazy but important and I remember them because they are vivid to my mom or my dad or my sister, and I'm able to fabricate a sort of collective memoriam:

From my mom

On the first day of fourth grade for me, first grade for Lucy, my family went early to school to meet with Lucy's teacher. Lucy and I sat at a group of desks and waited while my parents met with her. Another mother and daughter came in early and the mom guided her daughter to sit at the same desk group as ours. The mother asked me what my name was and then introduced me to her daughter. My mom walked over and chatted with the mom about how great the teacher was supposed to be, while Lucy and I ignored her daughter and laughed about how the group of desks had a name tag and was called "orange" and how none of the desks were orange. Mom turned to me and said, "Okay Cec, let's walk over to the fourth grade hall now!" We stood up and hugged Lucy goodbye. The other mother looked up, confused. Then, she looked at Lucy. As we walked out of the room, the mother told her daughter to get up and sit at another group of desks. My mom tells me she cannot forget that.

From VHS

My sister arrived into this world on June 8th, 1999. I too arrived at St. Luke's hospital in Bethlehem, Pennsylvania with a toy Elmo video recorder in hand. I was almost three. What I know from that day isn't from memory, rather from VHS tapes from my father's camcorder. A few summers ago, Lucy and I sat in my grandparents' living room and watched tapes after tapes of our childhood.

When we turned on "LUCIA KATHERINE STURMAN BIRTH 06/08/99", dimly shot on the camcorder, hazy and shuffling around in a hospital room, I felt my stomach drop and I immediately wanted to turn it off.

Because it became quite apparent that the star of Lucy's birth was me.

On film, I'm precious and hilarious; flirting with the camcorder as I'm bouncing around the hospital room with my short, platinum blonde bob. With my Elmo camcorder, I am also recording my baby sister's first moments in this world, and answering my dad's questions:

"Where are we Ceci?"
"The hospital for my new baby sister".
"Are you excited?"
"Yes, I can't wait, look!" pointing to my new white t-shirt that said "I'm a big sister"

Watching this was numbing.
I thought,
Thank God my dad focused that day on me. I looked over at my sister, eyes glued to the screen, watching this pure, innocent celebration in the moments of her birth permanently illuminated on tape by her gregarious big sister, and not the chilling silence of everyone else in the room.

The moment Lucy was born, something changed in all of us.

My birth

Mom went from work to the hospital, because it was the time. I was on the way. So right after everything, I was in her arms sleeping away. Ceci felt jealous that I had everyone's attention in the room, she got over it, and liked me. She had showed love in her heart towards me, knowing that I might be the sister she could be friends with forever. Mom and Dad had been told by the doctors their daughter in their arms had Down Syndrome. They were devastated and surprised to hear the news of me. Maybe that was why I took the attention from Ceci. I looked normal, but on the inside was where it was laying and building, little and little and little and little. I didn't seem like a Down Syndrome kid at birth, I was just a regular baby exactly like my parents and Ceci, and as a baby I myself was not realizing how I would look like later in life.

Enabled

We were drawn of the same gene pool, my sister
and I. Completely out of our own control, we are
called disabled and abled. So many times, we've
defined and redefined those words. I've been
endlessly humbled and broken by this
understanding.

Isolation

I wish I knew what Down Syndrome meant when I was
young
And clearly, I didn't.
I'm curious about it
I have questions all the time.
I know it doesn't define me
But, how can I stop the monster inside of me from
showing on the outside.

I have a gut feeling that people will take one
look at me and not like me at all.
I have questioned myself more than once and take
slow steps to understand me.

I try to know that is how God made me and
created gifts for me so DS won't even define me
at all.

I really don't like people taking one look at me
thinking: "We're just going to stare at you, if
you don't like it."

I know they're thinking "What's wrong with her"
and "Just look at her"

I can do nothing at all, just understanding that
is who I am.

From what they told me

I learned to walk
To the couch
After crawling for so long
I took my time
Just trying my best
One step at a time
Even though I fell on my butt
One time
That didn't stop me
To walk
I stood and walked to the couch
I felt proud of myself
For doing that
Then I crawled away
Thinking "Okay, I'm done."
That was the first
Time I walked
Accomplished
Bravery
Happiness
I felt those three words
In my head.

From Jack & Jill

We are in high school. Ninth and twelfth grades. Lucy and I share a bathroom. Both of our bedroom doors connect to our bathroom - I think the technical term for it is a "Jack and Jill" style bathroom. It's still painted this awful shade of baby blue that I picked when we first moved in. And although we have the potential to overlap a lot of bathroom time, we really don't. Lucy wakes up and gets ready much earlier than I do — she sets her alarm every night and wakes up the first time it rings whereas when I remember to set my alarm (usually begrudgingly around one or two in the morning) I press the snooze five to twenty-five times before I roll out of bed. Most mornings, mom comes in and yells at me. "Ceci. It is 8:30." She stopped reminding me that I needed to be at school by nine when she figured out it was not that I didn't know the time, rather I did not care.

Lucy wakes up, goes through her bathroom morning routine, and waits for me downstairs at the breakfast table from 8:30 until I rush downstairs, grab a piece of toast, and yell that we need to leave. She passively makes little sister-esque tattletale comments to Mom on a regular basis about my "disorganization problems", Mom tells me. Needless to say, my sister is much cleaner and much more organized in the bathroom (and in life in general). In the bathroom, her stuff isn't piled up or sprawled out recklessly, it's neatly organized in her cabinets, in which, she tells me, is where stuff is SUPPOSED to go. There are two separate sinks, so most of the time, we act like the other (messy, clean) side of the bathroom just doesn't exist.

One time, my told me he found it interesting that Lucy always closes her door to the bathroom and I always keep mine open.

I walked through our bathroom and opened Lucy's door. When she comes into my room, she always knocks on the door, regardless of the fact that it's always open.

"Hey girl."
"Hey girl."
"Do you want to give me some money for Mom's birthday present like we talked about?"
I sit on her bed and ignore her stare at the blankets I messed up.
"Yeah definitely."
"You know what I got her right?"
"The shirt right?"
"The BLOUSE, Lucy. It is much more than a shirt, girl, it's from Ann Taylor, it's very fahncy."
She laughs.
"So you can give me ten bucks if you want." I add.
She walks over to her closet, pulls out her very secret moneybox, full of One Direction and Selena Gomez articles and her eighth grade graduation certificate. She hands me a fifty — probably from her birthday, six months ago. Lucy is fantastic at saving money.
I reach for her money wad:
"All of it! Oh my goodness, Thank you." I grin.
She laughs again.
"Ceci...."
I wonder if she would give me all of it, though, if I persuaded her a little harder. Mom has this magnificent theory that I'm always out to take Lucy's money. Which isn't true, I'm just very curious about it.
"Come here, I'll grab you some change."
Lucy follows me through the Jack and Jill bathroom to my room. I ignore again, her wide eyes and raised eyebrows as she looks *for* my floor. I pick up my wallet from the ground and search through it for some change. After digging in a couple of jean pockets, I hand her a twenty and a ten. She takes it, without looking, and turns to go back. I stop her.

"How much do I owe you now?"

"Um" she tightens her lips and looks up at the ceiling. "$50 minus $10 is…" she counts back on her fingers.

"Lucy. You don't need your fingers for that. Fifty minus ten."

"Ceci, I use my fingers. That's how I learn. It's easier." She is upset now.

I pause and decide not to try and teach her something that would inevitably end up with her crying.

"It's 40." I say.

"Yeah okay, and how much did I give you?"

She counts on her fingers. "20, 21, 22..."

"Lucy. This is easy math."

She gets irritated. "40"

"No." I say sharply. "I gave you 30 dollars."

"Oh." She turns back to her room, annoyed.

"Lucy, I have to give you money, you don't care about your money?"

She faces me, "Ceci, stop."

I look at her for a long time. "I'll bring it to you later, I don't have it right now. Write mom a card."

I could see that I hurt her with my curtness. I thought about apologizing but I stopped myself short.

When I brought her the money later that evening,
I did.

"I am sorry for being harsh with you, girl." I
said. "I shouldn't have done that".

"I am sorry for not knowing how to count the
money." She replied.

"You don't have to apologize, you didn't do
anything wrong. Besides, counting is boring." I
smiled in concession.

"It is!" She laughed with me.

"I mean who cares about counting?"

From Jack and Jill, cont.

Blue and green walls
Of calmness (that I do believe for myself)
I like how it sets me to think of the ocean
It connects to my room and Ceci's
Jack and Jill is not how I would describe it
There's no sand, only two doors
To get to the other room
In this peaceful place
With two meanings of what organization means
The neat tidy side of having things where they
needed to be is mine
I think it's unique
But messy
Ceci's side,
Things being not being the same doesn't affect
that

I think of the ocean
Without the sand on the floor
To make our feet
Very weirdly uncomfortable on the toes
And between them

The bathroom has been connected
To the rooms
Since Ceci and I moved into the house
At a young age
We had our own version how our rooms should look
like
Our rooms matches our personalities so well
The attention grabber and entertaining was mine
Creative and sporty was Ceci's
Whenever she and I go to our rooms
The thoughts leave our minds
Of how our rooms look so different from each
other
Mouths shut to keep opinions closed.

From the rocks

You wake up to a pat on your arm.
Squatting down near your nightstand, he smiles
when you open your eyes
It's four in the morning, he whispers, as to not
wake your little sister sleeping soundly next to
you.
You look at him without words for a minute, you
debate if you really want to leave your bed,
which you don't, but your father, whom you have
made a promise to wake you up at this time, has
stuck to his side of the bargain.
Okay, you say.
He looks a little surprised, he smiles again.
Meet you outside in five. We have 20 minutes.
Five minutes later you are in your favorite
sweatshirt and you slip on your flip-flops as you
step outside.
You embrace your father, your glasses squished
against his chest, you breathe in the smell of
the mountains,
though you are at the ocean you will always
breathe in the smell of mountains when you are
with him.
He holds you, his strong hands hold tight.

I let go and silently we walk down the steps, we
walk past our neighbors' fences, we walk down
main street until we have reached the edge of the
town. We join dog walkers when we climb onto the
rocks
We find the spot we have claimed as ours years
ago
Where the rocks have flat backs for us to lean on
And we watch the sun rise and rise and rise until
the water is warm.
I curl up into my father's arms and we speak no
words but we hear each other loudly.

From the rocks, cont.

On the beach
In Rockport, Massachusetts
The scenery was beautiful
Very beautiful
The sun was shining perfectly
In the amazing blue sky
The rocks were fun to play in
Making towers, moats,
Covering our feet
The water felt nice on my feet
It was an incredible feeling
Playing about and about with excitement
It looked calm
And peaceful
And as I was on the rocks
I felt awesome and was able to move around
The best part was
Collecting the seashells
They looked beautiful
There were so many
I just couldn't find which one
I wanted
To take with me
And to keep
The many seashells
there
were just so beautiful

From I-95

A couple of years after we moved to Virginia from Pennsylvania, my mom and my sister and I took a trip up to Delaware to visit my mom's side of the family. I don't remember why, but for some reason my dad wasn't with us. Lucy and I sat in the backseat for the three hour trip.

I remember that Lucy somehow got away with eating too much pizza that day, and my mom was annoyed about it because it was basically inevitable that she would get sick* on our trip home.

Lucy has this thing with food.

Once, my mom, my sister, and I attended a picnic that some students in the community (or rather, their moms) initiated to facilitate a hangout between special needs kids and "normal" kids. My mom and I watched as all of the "normal" kids played kickball and all the kids with Down Syndrome spent the majority of the picnic making rounds after rounds to the food table, as their guardians, Mom and I included, desperately tried to regulate. It was kind of funny. Lucy didn't get sick* then but

another time, Lucy got sick* from eating seven slices of pizza two servings of taco salad and twelve brownies at our church potluck. What I've learned is that my sister, like other people with Down Syndrome, have very little self-control and ability to anticipate consequences for their actions. When Lucy has options, she wants all of it, over and over again. When people that aren't as familiar with DS politely ask me to explain what it is, probably expecting me to get all chromosomal, I resort to the potluck illustration.

So when I heard the first gag on that car ride, I was already prepared. I launched myself over the seat barrier, screaming and crawling up on the dashboard to avoid the spray. Lucy got sick* everywhere. Like, the back of mom's head, all over the books we were bringing back to Virginia from my grandma's house, all over our bags, all in the seats.

Mom, who deals with sickness* as poorly as I do, but realizing the family go-to-sick*-guy wasn't there, had to step up. As Lucy continued to explode, and I continued to scream in disgust, Mom gave me the nastiest side eye while soothing my poor sister. She pulled over at the closet gas station and yelled at me to get paper towels from the bathroom.

So I run in madly, apparently attracting concern because when I got out of the bathroom with paper towels in hand, the manager was waiting for me.

"Honey, are you okay? Where's your mom?"
"She's outside. My sister is sick*."
"Can you show me?"
"What? Uh, ok." We walk outside. "Mom, this lady wants to talk to you."
"Ma'am, is everything okay?"
She sticks her head out of the car where she has been rubbing my hunched over sister's back and looks up at the manager.
"Yes? My daughter is just sick, but it's okay. We just needed some paper towels."
I avoid my mom's eye contact as she stares me down, trying to understand what I brought about.

"Okay, we just have a policy whenever we see kids alone." The manager's eyes never leave Lucy.
"Right." My mom responds. "Ceci, go get more paper towels, did you really think three was enough?"

  *Lucy prefers the sickness to be vague, but she told me I could tell you at the end it was vomit

In the future

I would love to live with Ceci, I mean we always missed each other when she first went to New York to attend college. We had started a new chapter of our life that was too hard without seeing each other's faces. She's honestly someone to lean on and cuddle up with. As I said, I would love to live with her and let her be my guardian. When I first came in her life, I was the joy of her life and I have inspired her in many situations to come to God.

Over the years of being her sister, I always thought Ceci and I would live together and stick together as glue even when we go different ways. I never had had second thoughts about it honestly. As a sister of Ceci, I won't ever leave her side and let nobody take her away from me. As I said, we're like glue and glue stays together.

In the future, cont.

Lucy and I will live together sometime in the future when I need to take over as her legal guardian. Sometimes people ask me how I feel about this fact as if my answer is obvious and it is that I feel not great about it because it is somehow a burden. But that is ridiculous to me, I can't wait to live with my sister, to have endless sleepovers and dinners and lunches and breakfasts and grocery runs and gym dates with her. I am offended that she might not live with me. I am saddened by the circumstances that are necessary in order for me to take over, but I am never saddened by my sister's presence. Lucy will only ever add joy to my life. Only. Ever. Joy. Even in the mundane. When we are apart, we feel the separation immensely and endlessly; we always tell each other how much we miss each other, how we wish we could cuddle. We reunite, after months, weeks even, no matter if it is at our house in Virginia or the bus station in Washington D.C. or at a coffee house in Arusha Tanzania or San Francisco Airport, Lucy will unfailingly sprint up to me, jumping up to hug me and I will catch her. We don't let go for minutes.

I think that people might be concerned that my normal life and my normal future is somehow jeopardized by being Lucy's sister. I would answer that 1) we are all way too concerned about living a normal life and a normal future and 2) if there is ever a future path that won't allow me to be the best sister I can be, that's not normal and that's definitely not for me.

From Bethlehem

I grew up in Pennsylvania and lived there from when I was one to six years old. I was there because it was good for Ceci and me and our mom's church work. I knew my hometown was more than that to me (I call it home). I became a social butterfly and happy kid who loved being in the center of attention. I made people smile. I loved, loved my hometown and everything about it. I tried swimming lessons, which was fun, though it was not my strongest. I was a serious fan of the Disney princess Cinderella, she and the prince were my favorite… more than the step-mother, step-sisters, and cat (I love the film dearly every time I see it). Socializing was my thing and I loved doing that all the time, I was an expert at it. Being with my family was a blessing and I enjoyed spending time around them doing fun stuff. I used to be cute and beautiful (my natural hair color was better than it is now). I sympathized with my mom's and sister's feelings. Ceci and I began to create an emotional relationship with each other even though we had our fights. My best friend Sarah and I met in kindergarten. When I first met her, I knew she and I were going to be the best of friends and I liked her. She was an amazing friend to me at all times and I was the same to her. Home had brought me pop music, friends and people, my first starring role in a Christmas pageant, dance lessons, children's choir, etc. to make me to grow into the person I was becoming to be. I was born and raised and created in the hands of those who loved me and kept me rising up when I fell. No matter what I was becoming, I was the person over the years with a heart full of compassion and faced any obstacles along the way. My home, mom's work, and my fears of space heaters and sleeping in the dark slowly became a place with light I was brought to live and live and live.

From Dad
John Sturman

It was a clear fall morning in Bethlehem. I walked out of the house with Ceci and Lucy. It was a school day. Ceci had just turned five. Lucy was two, and had started walking only three months before, so it was an exciting time but there was a sense of unease in our family. It was Ceci's second week of kindergarten. She was quite anxious about this new chapter in her life. She had been in preschool for two years. The preschool was only a half-day and it was in the building where her mother worked. She also knew many of the preschool children from church, so spending time out of the house without me, or her mom, was not a big step for her. Kindergarten however was different and definitely a big step for her. We decided to pick an elementary school in our district that had a kindergarten with a strong program. This school, James Buchanan Elementary, was just outside of neighborhood. When we went with her on the first day, it was a group of 15 other kinder gardeners she did not know.

Ceci approaches new situations with both hopefulness and fear. Letting go of us to go into a room with a larger group of people new to her was not easy. There were tears. There were also moments when she would hug our thighs, not wanting to let go and cross into the big room of the unknown those first couple of weeks.

That morning, Ceci, Lucy, and I headed out through the back yard to the car and we drove to James Buchanan Elementary School. Ceci reluctantly left me to go into her classroom. This was a Tuesday and Tuesdays were teaching days for me at Rutgers University, so after school, she would go to the afterschool care instead of having me pick her up at lunch time.

Her mother and I both worried about Ceci and how much trouble she had adjusting.

It was a huge season of change for Lucy, too. People with Down Syndrome are born with very low muscle tone. This factor alone accounts for a number of challenges ranging from speech clarity, early fatigue, and coordination challenges. Lucy started physical therapy at only three weeks. Speech therapy, education therapy, and occupational therapy started soon after. We added music therapy when she was two. Most of these services were at home, but center-based services started after her second birthday. So even though she was only two, Lucy actually had a similar amount of "schooling". Lucy was very motivated to walk. When her muscles were too week to walk and she hadn't quite figured out crawling, she would roll herself from one side of the room to the other. She had been walking since June, right after her second birthday. When Lucy started walking, her physical therapist became a lot less appealing to her. So much of her physical therapy was based on getting her to walk. When her mobility exploded through walking, she didn't want to hold still for her therapist to help her develop greater strength and control. But this was a Tuesday morning, and she still needed work on her gait, so we returned home for physical therapist.

Our college student babysitter arrived. She reported to us that news was breaking in New York about a horrible plane crash involving the World Trade Center. So we turned on the TV. The story and horror snowballed in the coming minutes. I was planning to drive in to New Jersey that day. But it became clear that this was not a normal day. As the story was evolving, many of us wondered what would happen next. The class I was teaching at Rutgers that afternoon, and indeed all other classes that day, were cancelled. I worked from home in a distracted state. In these moments, we all want to have our family close to us. We called the school; James Buchanan Elementary did not cancel school. Still, I wondered whether to get Ceci and bring her home. I looked over to my other daughter, and realized that it was a normal day for Lucy as she explored her world. I let the babysitter go early and got Lucy to take a nap after lunch.

The day seemed to last a long time. Lucy and I went to get Ceci at the school at Four. I expected to meet Ceci in an anxious space. But she seemed pretty content and happy to see us. Lucy ran up to her with exuberance and gave her a big hug. Lucy's hugs have always been enough to brighten one's day. We gathered her things in the classroom and walked out to the car. Ceci turned to me as we were walking out and said "I met a new best friend today." I was thrilled that not only had she emotionally survived this big day, she met the girl who would be her best friend throughout elementary school.

We drove home without the radio on as Ceci recounted the day. As soon as Ceci brought her things into the house, I announced that we were going for a walk. It was still a gorgeous day. We walked out of the door and the girls got into our red wagon. I pulled them in the wagon past the library down Church Street. We turned right on Main Street. I was glad to see that our favorite ice cream shop in the neighborhood was still open. We stepped into Confetti Cafe and got ice cream cones. The girls enjoyed ice cream in the wagon. When Ceci finished her ice cream, she pulled Lucy in the wagon. We stopped at the playground and Lucy showed off her new mobility skills.

Elizabeth called to let us that the church she worked at was having a special service that night. She came home to a fast dinner. We talked briefly about the news. The girls of course were not able to let the gravity of the day in. We assured them that they would be okay, even though the world can be a scary place. I'm not sure if any of the words stuck. I am glad that I had the chance to walk around outside on a nice day and enjoy watching the girls play, it helped me feel okay.

The gravity of the day took a while to understand and Elizabeth and I did our best to keep the girls away from it. We avoided watching news on TV until the weekend. I quickly realized I had no words for myself that would make this better or help them make sense of it.

As I watched my girls play, I wondered what I would eventually have to say to them. Nothing would be the same, yet the news of the day was not as important that the love I had for my daughters. All of my decisions that day were simply based on the reality that love is more important than the hate that happened and that will continue to happen. If there are any good explanations or perfect words of comfort, I sure didn't have them. I just wanted them to know that no matter what, we would be there for each other.

I also felt like the people who wanted to hurt America on 9/11 would have the upper hand if we only dwelled in shock and grief. I remembered how the Grinch tried to steal Christmas but the residents of Whoville didn't let them, by choosing joy instead.

It brought my heart joy to watch the girls play at the playground, enjoy their ice cream, and ride around in our red wagon. I'm glad I chose to let them play over trying to explain the darkness in the world. Choosing love has always been the way I want them to live.

June 2016

For my whole life, I believed that my father was
unshakable. The man who could scale mountains.
Bike hundreds of miles. Travel across the world.
Teach engineering at a university. Quit his job
to be a stay-at-home father when my mom had the
opportunity to excel at work. Sit through nights
of his daughter's stomachaches and comb through
our hair when we got that terrible spell of lice
in 2007, and again in 2013. When I was young, I
used to complain that it would never snow on my
birthday, in late august. For my fifth birthday
he brought snow to our back-yard.

We depend on him.
and
I didn't let myself think that my dad could be
like me,
scared, vulnerable.

He had been working at a civil engineering firm
since we moved to Virginia 13 years ago. And
eventually, he became so good at his job that he
was promoted to a top position. His brilliance,
kindness, and ethical driven-leadership was
admired by everyone around him, except some guy
above him who was threatened. My mom and I are
convinced he is now replaced my dad with a
younger workaholic who won't take long lunch
breaks every other week to go to meetings about
Lucy's Individualized Education Plan, (IEP) and
is probably pretty lame.

So, when my strong, resilient, father got laid
off, it was the first time I've ever wondered if
everything was going to be ok with us. My family
suddenly became scared, vulnerable.

Not to mention this all happened the week before
Lucy's' birthday, everyone's favorite national
holiday.

Lucy always forgets mom's birthday is in January, so after mine in August, and Dad's in November, she starts announcing her birthday, which is "coming up next" in June. It starts off slow, but when March hits, it's a weekly reminder. When May hits, it's hourly.

"I'm going to be 17 in 20 days!"

"My birthday is in one week."

"Ceci can you believe it? My birthday is so soon."

To these reminders, we always jokingly reply, "Is it? Oh dang, I totally forgot, I thought your birthday was in July!"

To which she always replies, "Stop it guys".

Anyone who knows Lucy at all knows how important her birthday is to her. Many people know all about June 8th and lovingly shower her with gifts and shout-outs that day. Lucy even wakes up on her birthday mornings and texts everyone in her phone:

"Hello, it's my birthday".

Iconic, truly.

For me, that June was a transition period. Unsurprisingly, I didn't like it.

I thought that when I got back from my semester studying abroad, I would absolutely have a summer plan lined up, I would get one of the many, many internships (publishing, nonprofit, activist groups, etc.) to which I had applied, and I would definitely not be in Virginia, with my family.

But, there I was. I either didn't hear from or got denied by all the internships, didn't have an apartment in New York, and couldn't even get a job in Virginia. On top of this all, I spent all of my life's savings in Europe, so that summer I was completely broke, to the point where I couldn't even afford to do things with my friends from home. I basically sat at home that whole month half-heartedly applying for more internships, stress-working out twice a day at the gym my parents paid for, and catching up on shows on my freshman year roommate's HBO account. I would wait around until one of my family members wanted to go get food or do something outside the house.

I complained to mom about how bored I was every day, so she gave me a list of chores - clean out all the stuff in your old room, weed the garden, help Lucy with her summer school homework - which I complained about, and the cycle continued.

It wasn't until my dad got laid off that I really understood why I needed to be with my family that summer. I observed a shift, I felt like that week was the first time my parents saw me in a role other than daughter; it was the first time I felt like I had something significant to offer other than my existence.

The morning my dad got laid off, my mom called me incomprehensibly crying and I was convinced he was dead.

My dad came home at ten in the morning and sat on the couch for an hour with my mom, reflecting somberly. I watched them silently, and at noon, I made them lunch. They wanted to go on a prayer walk at a retreat center an hour away. They wanted me to drive. They said they couldn't drive. Later I picked up Lucy from school and kept her attention away from my parents, because we decided not to tell her, at least until her birthday frenzy was over. She wouldn't be able to handle it emotionally, we thought.

I made dinner.

That Saturday, I drove back from a sleepover at a friend's house at seven in the morning so that dad, mom, and I could clean out his office before Lucy woke up and noticed we were gone. We thought it would take about three hours and Lucy probably wouldn't wake up until one. We got to his office and his ex-office manager let us in. My mom sharply inhaled when she saw how much we had to do. We tore apart his office bookshelf by bookshelf; we sorted through shelves full of books and notebooks and papers and binders and pens and folders, his engineering licenses, 11 years' worth of national park calendars, old pictures of me in my soccer uniforms, old pictures of Lucy in her dance leotards, an award I won for best attendance in 3rd grade, cards we both wrote him for father's day.

And we waited as he slowly decided what was confidential information to leave behind, what could be recycled, and what he wanted to take home. These were his projects, work he was proud of. My mom, who would have usually been less patient about his slow indecision, pushed on silently, occasionally leaving to cry in the hallway because she couldn't bear to see the pain he was in.

I sat too quietly and as I sorted through all of the stuff, it was hard not to think about my fathers' father and all of his stuff.

I thought
Wasn't this the same stuff my grandfather was addicted to collecting, that he refused to throw away, refused to let my grandmother throw away, even as his piles took over rooms and garages and driveways to the point that my grandmother was embarrassed to invite anyone over but us for the past ten years, wasn't this just the same

stuff that,
in just three months could finally be freed?

In just three months
stuff that we would be faced with the impossible
task of sorting, no one to stop us anymore.
Clearing out boxes and boxes, for hours, for
months to follow with silent rage and confusion,
sadness mostly. My parents fought because my
father struggled to let a lot of his fathers'
stuff go too.

Lucy would approach me quietly, in one of those
silent months, and ask when the stuff would
finally be over. I miss dad, she told me.

In his office that day
I wondered if my dad was going to be just like
his father. But this stuff was different right,
it? It matters. I wondered if it all mattered to
my grandfather at some point. I didn't know him
like that. I didn't want my father to become like
his father but I don't know how he could escape
it.

I wondered if I too, would become just like my
father and my father's father. It was hard not to
think about the stuff that I, too, am unable to
let go of. Whether it is in my mind or whether I
can touch it. It all matters and I cannot let it
not matter even if I want to.

I thought about where I have come from. What I
keep with me. I wonder if I can ever escape it.
I think that was the summer I learned that I'm
not alone.

We packed the car and the next day, my father,
mother and I put on a party for Lucy, one of our
best, yet.

From Berkeley

So many memories
As an infant
On and off the plane
Into the nice breeze of the fresh air
Going to see nana's and grandpa's house
Seeing many gorgeous sights of sunsets
Spending time with family friends and
Creating great times
I loved the atmosphere of it
The night skies were so peaceful I could
Sleep on my dad's shoulder
Every trip is amazing
I now see everything with eyes wide open
A good interest and
Nature's beauty
Having the best family time
I like the lights, I could see so much color
Berkeley California
A place of happiness
Light never fades
It shines.

From Berkeley, cont

ICY CITY spit me out
    ignite her
    LIVE her

Hip-notize, then tease her
Slap her sound awake
        So she'll never see dawn
                She won't get where she's going
                Until she's long gone
And she'll sweat through
The clothes that never kept her warm

Don't tell her about the sun, ICY CITY
You are jealous, too.
So don't let her stay long

        Drive her north, driver
        Quick! Before pink cheeks and golden eyes
steal her in
        The freckles are useless here.
    North we will go.
                Defiant, adolescent, irresponsible,
                Stay, stuck and wrong.
Drive through the night
See that storm? That's it. Go.

You chose this, you bought this dampness over
    The shelter of your parents
        The ICY CITY the pink freckles
    But damp is the shelter of your parents
As sweet as it is

You race where they rejected
    You force it to know you better
        Hold you tighter
            Make you kinder
                You spit it out faster

From imagination

I was young enough to come up with a world that
was different than the real world. I did it all
the time, which was driving mom and dad crazy.
They thought that was a problem and didn't seem
like something I should do. Would a kid without
Down Syndrome do that? Will people look at my kid
a little strangely? How is she focusing on this
when she needs real friends not fake ones? All
questions they had in mind. It was so unusual for
them to see me do this. I call this world "My
little world", because it is, and there's no
reason at all why it wouldn't be. Mom calls it
"Made up world". I had IMAGINARY FRIENDS, not a
problem to me,
but I have learned real friends are better.

From imagination, cont.

I keep thinking that one day I'll get back to it,
she says and laughs softly.

I look up to the words that haunt me and I see
they take shape in the form of a tall woman in a
long black coat and a very sleek briefcase. She
is talking to a man, it seems as if they have
just ran into each other on the C train to
Manhattan and are perhaps long time acquaintances
but have not seen each other in a while.

To starting a band? He asks. He has long blond
hair, longer and smoother than mine.

Yeah, she says.

How long have you played drums again?

Six years, she said.

He then begins to talk about himself, perhaps on
his own creative journey which I feel is obvious
given not only the long hair but the superhero
shirt under his plaid blazer but I cannot listen
anymore because I have heard all the universe
wants me to hear.

I thank it for giving me a break from my anxiety
about the train delays and being late to the
first day of my new gig.

The last time I heard the words that haunted me
they took form in my cab driver in San Diego who
told my mom that he desperately and only ever
wanted to be a comedian but he was going to
nursing school to make money first. Eventually he
would get back to it, he told her as I sat
silently in the cab like I always do.

These words haunt me but I don't know if it is because they tempt me or they disgust me. I have heard these words come out of my mouth on so many occasions that perhaps I own them more than my own creative passion.

If I could only sit across myself on the subway and watch myself scribble notes desperately before they fell away from me and think, I hope she is living to her deepest passions, I hope she is not instead desperately lining up twelve step-by-step alternative plans and scenarios and gigs because she does not trust that living to her deepest passions could ever sustain her.

Blank minds

Once I think
About something
It's there
Then it goes away for some reason
My mind feels like it's empty inside

For a second
So I try to get back in the thought
Not all works as I imagined it would
5, 4, 3, 2, and 1
Work, my mind
Where's the thing you want to get out
Get it out
Right now
I feel like you're not letting me focus here
I can't seriously figure out what in the world
That I can't use it now
I need to use it
Get it together
I don't need to have blank minds
At this moment (can you relate)?

From pain

I was in ninth grade and sitting at the lunch
table across from a girl who had absolutely no
idea what to do or how to comfort me after I hung
up the phone and said, "Well, my grandma's dead
now."

She said, "You're not going to stay at school
today, are you?"
"I guess I am," I said.

I didn't cry about her death for weeks and the
first time I cried was at her funeral when her
best friend Edna testified that she still can't
believe her best friend, her travel buddy, had
died. They had been planning to go to Asia and I
was so sad that Edna could never go to Asia with
her best friend.

Later, much later, I would mourn the most loving
woman in my life leaving my life, too. I would
never be able to sit on her lap and have her rub
my back and tell me funny stories about my
mother. I would never be able to tell her about
my sadness and hear her tell me it was going to
be okay and actually believe her, because she
felt it too.

When Lucy and I were younger, Grandma Delsie
would drive us to the mall in Allentown and buy
us whatever we wanted even though she had barely
any money and my dad would ask her to please
stop, we didn't need toys, she needed to save
what little she had. My mom would just sigh and
say that this is how she is, John. This is how
she will always be. My dad asked her to stop
buying us candy and she would say, John I can't
help it, we were learning "C's" today.

She always defended me when mom or dad scolded
me, she always told them to go easier on us, we
were only kids.

She only ever raised her voice at me once, when I
was freaking out because I couldn't decide what
stuffed animal to buy at the Disney store and we
were holding up the entire line. I couldn't
believe that I hurt the woman who could only love
me.

I'm so sorry grandma, don't be mad. I'm so sorry.

Later,
Mom, does she hate me?

Ceci, She could never.

From pain, cont.

I was in the 6th grade when dad broke the news to
   me. I had just come home from Stone Hill Middle
   School. I felt my heart began to break, I broke
   down in tears. I thought "What, how could this
   happen to me?" I had never imagined my grandma
   would go into the last stages of her life like
this. I thought to myself "she's going to make it
   so she could stay alive." I wanted her to stay
      alive; she's my grandma (my mom's mom). As I
listened to the words "your grandma died" from my
   dad's mouth, I said, "she can't die like this"
   between my cries. Dad could tell I felt so, so,
so devastated to hear the news. He knew how much
I loved her, and how I was going to miss her hugs
   so much. My grandma was everything to me from a
young age. She was my happy place. I was a crying
      mess, my heart just withering away from the
sadness I felt that she was no longer alive. But
   I knew she was in my heart and speaking in my
   ears. I always kept thinking and thinking and
   thinking to myself "When will I see my grandma
                                    again?"

There has always been much deep seeded pain and darkness on my mom's side of the family, and Grandma Delsie seemed to be the only glue that could hold us together.

When we lost her, we lost almost everyone

and it is only now that I recognize my mom's youngest sister and her boys as a vital extension of my immediate family, it is only now I feel grave significance about reconnecting with my cousins

but with my grandparents on my dad's side distant, for many years it seemed as if I only had my mom and my dad and Lucy.

Separation

When I didn't know why I felt pain I took my pain
out on my sister. And my dad. And my mom. And my
close friends. But mainly my sister; she was the
easiest victim, the most undeserving and the
least likely to fight back.

I told my therapist that I felt very disconnected
with the girl I once was; the violently angry
girl, who probably feels very disconnected with
the mostly soft, sensitive people pleaser and
nervous self-sacrificer I am now. My therapist
told me that I am very much that girl. We feel
the same emotions, we just understand them
differently.

A couple of years ago I asked Lucy to forgive me
for how I treated her when I was young. She did,
of course, on the spot. She told me that she

didn't remember me being mean to her, but she
does remember crying a lot around me:

                                    Making me cry

        It is one of my biggest regrets, my anger

                                        Hurting

Both of us, I would. Hurt.

        Fall to my knees and cry,

    *Yelling at me, which I hadn't imagined hearing
                                from her mouth*

        I don't want to hurt you. Why am I hurting
us?

    *I didn't know what to do or how stop myself from
                                crying so much*

            I am sorry

            that anger I will never be able to
        take back.

    *I do forgive you and I just want us to become
                            closer to each other*

College

The decision came almost whimsically. Decisions have always been hard for me, but this one somehow wasn't. I read somewhere when we put deliberation and thought into short term, less weighty decisions, we are generally satisfied with the outcome. Long-term decisions are totally different; deliberation and thought doesn't produce satisfaction. For long-term decisions, it's generally better to rely on our gut.

And that's exactly how my college decision came. From intuition that didn't even make sense to me at the moment, and really, still doesn't.

I applied to 11 schools across the country and it came down to one in Virginia that half of my high school was going to, one in California that was lovely and would make me very tan but was entirely too expensive, and one in New York City that I'd never heard of and my dad made me apply to because it had a good English program and a free application, which took me approximately 10 minutes and I didn't even submit my writing sample which was arguably the most attractive part of my application. I visited the New York City school for the first time in April after I was accepted and didn't really like it, but decided right then and there I was supposed to go there. So, I did.

Decisions are hard for me, but transitions are much worse.

I had such a hard time leaving my parents when it was time for me to go to Kindergarten, that every single morning(until May, my mom says emphatically)when they dropped me off to my Kindergarten class, I clung to their legs and cried, for hours sometimes. This concerned my parents, my birthday just hit the cut-off date for Kindergarten, but I was younger than the rest

of my classmates, maybe I was too young. My
teachers were concerned I was too immature.
Eventually, I would catch up and be placed in
programs for advanced learners that would assure
my parents that they didn't do me a disservice by
sending me to Kindergarten early.

When I was eight, and my parents told me that we
were moving from Pennsylvania to Virginia because
my mom landed a new job — to be senior pastor of
a new church-development in a soon-to-boom-but-
never-really-boomed suburb of Brambleton,
Virginia — I was inconsolable. For, again, about
a year. This lasted from the moment they told me
we were moving and I immediately burst into tears
and ran to the land-line to call my best friend,
to the day we started packing our things, to the
day we arrived at our new house, to about one
year into living in our new house, when I finally
made a friend and decided it was probably going
to be okay.

I hated my parents for usurping me from my
happiness, I hated my sister for not being as
upset as I was about it. I was so angry, my
parents remind me, that every night when my dad
came home from work, I would run up to him and
hit him and beg him to fight me. He would often
wrestle me to the ground and pin me there for a
few minutes or so, until I was too tired from
fighting and would give up. It was around then
that my parents decided it was a good idea to
sign me up for every sport they possibly could.

My parents also remind me that little transitions
were hard for me too; even small changes like
moving from soccer team to soccer team, or moving
from middle to high school were borderline
traumatizing. Somehow, the anger I experienced in
my youth faded out into my teenage years
(manifesting more significantly in nervousness
and defensiveness, sometimes meanness) and I

learned how to avoid significant transitions that
would ruin me,
so the next big move for me was when I was 18,
when I moved to college.
Actually, it moved me.

> The Morning is the first thing I feel
> A punch in the gut
> Grief where there could be
> Should be
> Relief
> A gut in the punch
> The mourning is the first thing I feel

I wrote this poem in the first semester of my
freshman year. It was the first time I started
actually writing poetry because I wanted to and
not for a school assignment. I've later come to
understand this period as the true genesis of my
creative passion.

I was depressed. Anxious. Confused. Trying to fit
in and tragically failing. Seeking attention from
the wrong people. Missing home. Missing my
friends. Hating my school. Feeling free. Feeling
alone. Able to own the world in a way I never
had. Able to explore. I became independent.

For a year, every single morning I woke up
anxious. I felt empty, I felt tense. I felt like
I could cry at any minute.

I have gone through this feeling many times
throughout my life, for a variety of lengths, but
this year was by far the hardest. No matter what
I did the night before, no matter what I had
planned for the day ahead, no matter what time I
woke up, I would feel this way. It's not as if I
didn't have friends around and I didn't have a
metro card granting me entrance to the most
exciting city in the world. I had permission to
skip class for concerts in Harlem, to spend my
Saturdays at food festivals in Williamsburg, to

read a book all afternoon on a park in Greenwich Village and pretend to be anyone I wanted to be. No one could tell me otherwise. I had all of that. I just had nothing, too.

It started with my father's aura of conclusion. Although I knew it was just his anxiety about getting on the road back home (theirs, not mine anymore) I was angry that he wanted to leave me. Later when we embraced for the last time, my tears would leave wet spots on his chest, to his surprise. But I ignored him as I stalled through empty talk of the weather with my mother, standing on the long staircase outside of my new dining hall, watching students mingle on their way out, in pairs of two or three, laughing. I wondered if they just met, if they were roommates. When I thought about my new room the swelling deep in my stomach crawled to my throat. My mother's eyes the same color as mine brimmed with tears, for her own sadness and for anticipation of my own. My sister stood in silence and listened to us talk about the clouds, looming and grey.

The moment my parents left me off at the school cafeteria, literally the moment we said goodbye, I burst open. After they left, I ran downstairs to the bathroom of the school cafeteria, a dreadful place I would come to know well later, and cried.

I cried there for 30 minutes, desperately begging my body to resolve itself, until another girl finally came in to the bathroom. She looked at me with knowing, sad eyes. "Are you okay?"
Yes, I smiled and forced a laugh. It's okay.

"It's going to get better, I promise".
That girl, I would come to see on campus, I would
come to know her name, she was popular actually,
she was a star on the track team. I always
wondered if she remembered that.

I started calling my mom a few weeks in.
I'm not doing okay.
She was worried, but she said it was normal.
She told me she felt empty too, without me, they
all did.

She told me that Lucy would lay in my bed and
cry.

It's going to be okay, she told me.

When my mom visited me about a month in and we
met at Rockefeller center, I was bubbling and
bubbling and as soon as I saw her I burst open
again. I held her and cried in front of hundreds
of strangers. As we sat in a diner, I told her I
wanted to transfer, I made a terrible mistake, I
hated this place.

She told me it was going to be okay. But that I
should stick it out through the semester. If I
really felt that way in the spring, I could
transfer.

I held on to that promise desperately.

When she left, I burst wider. I found a church to
sit in and cry. Every Sunday I went to that
church and I cried because I could not imagine
that I would ever feel better and I wanted to be
close to my mom and I wanted God to notice me —
to save me.

I hated myself for not being able to adjust
normally, to enjoy college like it seemed like my
high school friends did, to enjoy college like it
seemed like I was on instagram.

But I needed to come to terms with the truth
about myself.

The poems I wrote, about my feelings, for the
first time ever, felt good. They felt valuable,
they felt worth something.

For some reason, I again, still don't understand,
I decided to stick it out until the spring, and
when the weather got better, I felt a little
better too.

My sister would call me, she would text me, she
would tell me she missed me so much, she would
cry when she saw me. My parents would tell me how
much she missed me.

When I saw her in person, when I went home, she
shut me out. She was cold.

I was back, I was invading her space now. I was
taking the attention.

Like when she my sister was first born and I got
over my initial excitement, realizing she was
here to stay.
I was so jealous of this new creature that once
my parents caught me leaning over her crib with a
pencil "to poke her eye out" (a story Lucy will
never let me forget.

Lucy adjusted to being the center of attention
and when I came back she did not like to share it
with me, not at all.

She would sit in silence at the dinner table as I
told my stories, she would ignore me throughout
the house, she would tell me nothing was wrong
when I asked, she would close her door to our
Jack and Jill bathroom, she would freeze when I
embraced her.

This is quite strange, Mom and Dad would tell me, don't take it personally, she just doesn't know how to properly process these emotions.
The second I would be on the bus back to New York, she would text me that she loves me so much and misses me so much, and I would be confused.

This happened every time I came home for about three years, and over time, it got better, but every time it hurt. Both of us.

I left her. I betrayed her.

We were made for each other and I broke us.

College, cont.

When Ceci left for college, I felt very devastated that I wasn't going to be with her, face-to-face. Whenever she comes home from college, she feels like I'm not always the chatty Lucy, but I felt like she had hurt my feelings by going to college. I was super excited for her, I was worried how I would feel and how my reaction was going to be like. Over the years, Ceci had always stayed by my side and made feel so inspired. I kept thinking and over and over, "I want to be like Ceci."

I was 15 years old when Ceci left for the first time, I remember that day. I didn't want her to leave my side and felt like I wanted her to stay. I haven't recovered from crying the month of September that year. Why did she do this to me? I mean Ceci was the smartest person I knew and her kind words to me always made me want to do the same.

Still, whenever Ceci leaves to go to travel the fun places I would love to see the sights of and soak in how beautiful they are, I'm super jealous because my parents let her go and they don't let me.

We miss each other so much when we are in our different places. We communicate through phone calls, text messages, and FaceTime. She does visit me and I have visited her three times in her new home New York City. We are closer than we have been since when we younger. We don't fight now. Only playful fights.

No matter what Ceci will always be my sister. She graduated from St. Johns. She's 22 years old and she is doing so well rocking the age. Her smile is a wonderful thing about her I admire so much. Now that I'm 19 years old, when she comes to visit I run up to her and jump like a little kid

would, just without those rosy cheeks and
pigtails I used to have.

So so small without you

Lucy,

Am I doing this for you? Like I say I am?

Lucy,

Will you be okay without this? Without me?
Rather, separate the two, teach me how to.

Lucy, will I be better once I do this for you,
for me?

Lucy, I am scared that you are a shield and I am

So so small
Without you.

I am me. I am you, Lucy.

Release me, Lucy. You have always been forgiving.

Be forgiving once again.

Family

I couldn't ask for a better family, because I'm glad I get to inspire them as much as I can. My mom is a wonderful inspiration and role model. My dad is so supportive and motivating. My sister is very loving and warm-hearted. I love every person in my family, like my Grandma, Aunts, Uncles, Cousins, and Grandparents. I am so glad that my family is the most amazing in the world I could be blessed with. I love them all very much with all my heart.

Italy

*Ceci got to go to Italy. You went to visit Ceci
in Italy and left me.*

Like any younger sibling, my sister is quite
cognizant of any slight difference in parenting
that could be potentially be considered
favoritism.

*Ceci gets to drive
not well, clearly, because she wouldn't sit in
the front seat with me for two years after I
started
Ceci gets to go to college
before she started attending classes at the local
community college
Ceci gets to have a boyfriend
not any keepers evidently
Ceci gets to dye her hair
yes and now it's dead
Ceci gets to be in a band
Ceci also gets to be poor*

*Ceci got to go to Italy. And you went to visit
Ceci in Italy and left me.*

My mother and I sit in Florence at a cafe we have
been to two times already that day.
It is French, and we are both drawn to it more
than any other place in the town, which must say
something about our Italian bloodline.
I am comfortable with my mother, more so than I
have been in a while, but I am not at internal
ease because of a passive conflict that's been
festering in Rome with my study abroad mates and
my inability to clear it up before coming to
Florence. I wish it didn't affect me, but this
type of stuff always will. My body can move but
my mind stays.
stuck.
My mother sits with me and she knows I am not at
ease and she doesn't try to rationalize it for me
anymore, she just sits with me.

My mother's intuition is crazy. It always has
been.

I don't tell her my secrets because I know she
already knows them. Sometimes, I think that I
cannot have a private thought without her, and
that scares me. Sometimes, I am angry that I am
so predictable to her. For many years that anger
pushed me far away from her.

On this day in Florence, it marks two weeks
together in Italy, and she is leaving tomorrow to
return to my father and Lucy in Virginia. I am
anxious about this conflict and I am much more so
mad at myself because I cannot bring to the
forefront of my mind how much I will miss her,
even though it is swelling inside.

> *Ceci got to go to Italy. You went to visit Ceci*
> *in Italy and left me.*

We are in Vatican City now.

Sitting on two refurbished wine barrels in a
dimly lit wine bar in Vatican City across from

her apartment, romantic Italian music plays as we laugh together. The waiter gives us a bottle of Tuscan red when we asked for just two glasses and we decide not to correct him. We have always laughed together, even in the ugliest seasons of our relationship, laughter has been conciliatory. We both resort to laughter in uncomfortable situations and the laughter only eggs each other on further. But we are laughing because we are silly this evening and not uncomfortable.

My mother twirls her small silver hoop earring back and forth with her finger. She brings her hand to her neck and feels the shape of her clavicle every few minutes. As we finish our bottle, we remember silly times. There are many of them. Mostly about our silly, silly Lucy. We love her so much.

I feel my chest soften and I know that I am feeling what must be pride leaving myself as I think tender things about my mother like:

She is beautiful

She is kind

She is right

She has always been right

I want to be as strong as she is

Things I always knew but were so hard for me to release.

Things that suddenly meant so much more than her harshness and how much she expected of me.

The first time I took therapy seriously, my therapist suggested to me that I was preventing my own healing because I refused to work on my relationship with my mother. I refused to soften.

When I was young, maybe four or five, my parents found me standing in my room with a blanket tied around me as a mock-robe, holding my Children's Bible. I was commanding the attention of my stuffed animals, all sitting and lined up in order of importance on the ground in front of me. Little Dipper, the Dalmatian my grandma bought me at the mall, was front and center, recovering from a pretty serious scissor haircut. I was reading out of the Bible and telling my stuffed animals about God's love for them.

I wanted to lead the crowd, to be as smart, to love God as much as my mother, my role model.

And as we left that wine bar, with the help of the wine of course, I dropped my guards and told her things that I kept from her in high school. I told her about the parties, about Prom night, about things that hurt me. She listened and she raised her eyebrows at a few details, but of course, she knew it all. She wasn't angry like I was convinced she would be. She was waiting for me to tell her. And I was waiting to tell her.

As we walked together to our dinner reservation across the river, I tripped on cobblestone and fell on my face, with the help of the wine of course.

I looked up, surprised, as my mom flopped over and laughed and laughed. I laughed too. A group of Japanese tourists alarmingly looked at each other as they watched the scene unfold.
Stupid Americans.
Stupid Americans healing.

There is no one that knows every inch of me so deeply and still loves me so deeply. I know she is my mother and she is forced to love me but I think that she could choose to love me less and she doesn't.

Papa

Sometimes there's comfort and helping out. Most of the time it is just hugging, a few "get down here and work on your assignments," and us just spending time together.
He sees things in a different way than I do. I talk about celebrities and he seems to care, since they make me happy. He ends every prayer by saying "Thank you for how she is beautiful, kind, and smart." I think to myself, "Just pray normally dude." When he does something and I say "dad, dad, dad, John, Johnny," I get annoyed he doesn't respond quickly to me and he tells me "Could you say that again" when he gives me attention and I think "Oh great, I have repeat myself again." I tell him, "I hate repeating myself" (it's my pet peeve). I love him, he loves me (I know), but it feels like, to me, there's a spark missing to showing the "I love you" between us. I mean, over the years of being in his life, he sees me as a baby girl who needs to know and understand and take more seriously the world that is in my little hands. I know for myself it might take me a little time to see it with my own eyes, I have eyes that have the word "Future" in them. He can tell I see that, but he always comes in and tells me "This blah, blah is a good opportunity for you and your skills to use for it." In that moment, I'm the person thinking, "I want to do my own thing, I appreciate what you're doing, but I'm at an age and I need myself to focus on the world at hand, I'm not fast, I'm taking my time, so, so please let me chose for myself what I see myself doing." My relationship with him has been overprotective (that's what he does) and I need for him to let me protect myself.

MBTI

All four of us have always been into understanding connections between ourselves and other people, especially through Carl Jung's Myers Briggs Type Indicator test that categorizes people into one of sixteen personality types. Jung believed that everyone fits into one of these 16 types, a coding mechanism which assigns you to four letters (it has since been updated a few times to assign more than four but most people still stick to the four).

According to this test you can be an E (extrovert) or I (introvert), N (intuitive) or S (sensor), T (thinker) or F (feeler), and P (perceiving) or J (judging).

Perhaps my family is attracted to this sort of metric because we are all N's ('intuitives' - people who seek to make deep connections and understand things in layers and dynamics and trends, rather than S's, or 'sensors' - people who take the world more literally and finitely, more so through the tangible five senses).

I know it is dangerous to think in absolutes, but I've found this mechanism to be quite accurate, and much more so than other categorizations (even though I quite identify as a Virgo).

I mention this because it is important to understand my family and how we understand ourselves, through our MBTIs.

Lucy: ENFJ
Ceci: INFP
Elizabeth: ENTP
John: INFP

We take the test at least once a year, and it barely ever changes. Sometimes I am an extrovert. Mostly I am not.

My mom and Lucy are extroverts who get their energy from being around people:

I'm a people person. I learn with visuals. I'm an energetic kid. I liked making friends easily and being so fun in many ways. These things make an extrovert. I have always been one since I was young.

My dad and I are introverted and enjoy drawing our energy from solitude (my dad quite a bit more so than me).

We are all N's, our only collective commonality. Then, the F/T breakdown indicates that the primary way in which the most of us respond to the world is through feeling, except for my mom, for which it is thinking. The P/J breakdown indicates how we organize the world around us, and for my parents and myself it is by pursuing adaptability and flexibility and for Lucy it is through having structure and organization. She keeps us in check.

All of us

Ceci was the first born child and she was raised in California like my dad. I was the second born child and was raised in Pennsylvania like my mom. A lot of people says she and I look alike which I don't see. Over the years in Ceci's life right before I came into hers, she had our parents wrapped around her little fingers. and wanted to become the only child in the family. Her and dad seemed alike in mom's opinion, the face and the personality. She was the sporty one in the fam exactly like my dad. I'm the fashionista one exactly like my mom. Ceci's personality and mine are different and unique.

Dad and Ceci are similar as I just mentioned, just how their personalities are similar. They're outdoors people, introverted, open-minded, funny, smart, and thoughtful. They're also great hikers you would love to hike with. Just when see them together, you see similar features and feel like "They look the same." I love both of them.

Mom

Mom has always been the person with good advice.
Her hugs give me joy when she wraps her arms
around me and says,
"God has given you the ability to be yourself and
you need to find anything that can define you."

Mom and I have personalities that are almost the
same. She and I love fashion, being organized,
generous to people around us. We're also
extroverted and our music choice is kinda
similar. We share the love of pop. We're
basically like sisters.

She inspires me so much and confronts me when I'm
sad and understands how I feel whenever there's
something on top of my mind. She and I have got
to know each other's feelings and I tell her,
"Mom, I know the look in your eyes, tell me
what's me wrong."

She knows in that moment I want to know.
Over the years, she got to know that her baby
girl, taking her life step by step, stands for
what she believes in, and is an advocate for
herself even though she has Down Syndrome. Plus
that she understands the real world and the need
to improve it that much more. Years and years
together, we have shown the world who I am and
who she is and always come together when
something is wrong.

One night I said, "My gut has a feeling when I
get a job and that person (manager of the job)
will take one look at me and say "We don't want
you because you have DS."
Mom told me "American Eagle doesn't do that." I
said, "My gut tells me - that's how I feel."
Mom quickly knew that's how I felt and sided with
me, coming to my defense so her confrontation
would show.

She and I have stood by each other in many situations like that, the word love comes out of nowhere and brings us together.

Unmothered

Perhaps there was an event
only my body, not I, remembers:
this that chokes and blinds me
often and soon again
I wait for it longingly.

Sweet sound, young breath
not yet familiar
to my ears of one language,
say it again
lips that move me.

Then I lose my sight,
I know what is next.
Where my head meets my body
caught, swollen, uncontrolled
compelled.

And because I prefer prose on death
doesn't mean I desire
the end

yet I seek it, too.

I think I am jealous of the girl
recently unmothered
who deserves to feel this harmony
and will, for longer than
the length of a hymn.

Papa, cont.

A few years ago in the summer I was running in my
neighborhood, like I usually did, listening to
music, like I usually did.

It was before a car hit me on my bike, and I
could still use my ankle properly.

I was running on a main street and a man on a
bike pulled up next to me licked his lips and
started talking to me, following me. I did not
want this man to talk to me or follow me but he
did and he did more faster so I ran faster and
searched for the closest store to run into.

This is not unusual for girls running or walking
or even just breathing, and this type of thing
had happened before, so after I escaped him, I
continued my run. I turned down another street
and was soon approaching a group of construction
workers. My stomach dropped in nervous
anticipation but I decided I must be bold and run
by them without assumption. As I got closer I saw
a woman construction worker was part of the group
and a part of me calmed.

But still, one of the men starting making groping
motions to me as I ran by and they all burst into
laughter. As I held my breath and ran faster I
made eye contact with the woman, who was laughing
too.

There was something about the way that woman
betrayed me that broke me down. As soon as I
turned the corner I burst into tears.

I called my father and I told him what happened.

At first he was quiet.

Oh Ceci. Are you okay? I am so sorry. I am so
sorry this must happen to you.

It's fine dad, it's not just me.

It's not fine, it's not just you.

You know, you should write a letter to your local congressperson, he told me. You can do something about this. I will help you write it.

He became angrier.

This is so disgusting, he told me. I could feel in his silence his anger.

My dad does not anger easily.

I love you Ceci, I'm so sorry.

He later sent me all of the contact information for my congresswoman.

Over the years I have received surprise packages from my father in the mail.

Pepper spray. Reflective bike vests. Bike lights. My Virginia ballots and voting information (he convinced me early on that my vote matters so much more in Virginia than in New York). Figs. Clif bars. My favorite conditioner. A bike bell. Endless articles on bike safety.

When I had my bike accident, I wasn't wearing a helmet.

He was the first person I called when I was sitting on the side of the road, surrounded by a crowd of witnesses screaming questions at me. WE SAW HIM. WE CALLED THE POLICE. ARE YOU OK. GET HER RUBBING ALCOHOL NOW. I can't think. I have to talk to my father, I told them. And when I told him I was hit by a car, he yelped.

He didn't lecture me until after he was sure I was safe and going to be okay. But in his next package he sent my "bike safety ID card" - a laminated piece of paper with my eight year old smiling self in a helmet taken after a week-long safety class my father and I attended in Bethlehem.

I let her down too.

I learned to ride on a tandem bike, behind my father.

Two years ago we rode 50 miles together through West Virginia. He could have gone for 100, he told me later (and I absolutely could not have) but it would not have been fun without me.

My father is my greatest and most trusted friend. He is healing and thoughtful and kind. He is soft like I want to be.

In good, we both love nature and activity and contemplative exercises like meditation and yoga and writing and tortilla chips and building others up and believing things can be better than they are.

In bad, we are both often trapped in our own minds and insecure and entirely too self-sacrificing.

We know our weaknesses and we hold each other accountable to going outside of our comfort zones.

He continues to challenge me and grow me, to learn patience and kindness, to remember when I get very mad about men that I cannot be mad at them all.

Mom, cont.

I'm naming my daughter Elizabeth, after you.

Lucy often tells my mom this.
My mom will smile and say, that's sweet Lucy.

Lucy wants to be a mother so bad.
So bad.
When she's 44 she will get married and have
children, she tells us.

Lucy is boy-crazy. she falls in love daily and
often. She crushes on boys in movies, bands, in
her classes, waiters that are nice to her, my
friends. She is unabashed about it too - giggling
and hugging, talking in a voice three octaves
higher than normal.

It's annoying but it's cute.

I'm not sure if Lucy will be a mother. Over the
years, many people, including her own family
members have told her she cannot. But I don't
want to tell her she cannot anymore. She deserves
to desire it. To feel like the woman she is. She
deserves to create another human out of her own
magnificence, to love it more than she has ever
loved anything else, to feel proud of herself for
it.

She deserves to appreciate my own mother so much
by naming her daughter after her.

In many ways, she would be an incredible mother.
She is such a natural caregiver, so warm and kind
and loving and comforting, so much more than me.

Crush

You had your eyes on me
When I was sitting with my friends at lunch
While you sat with your friends as they were
discussing a group assignment
You saw angels in my eyes
As I read my favorite poem out loud
You began to feel like you liked me
You felt your cheeks begin to blush
You couldn't help but overhear my angelic voice
That next day I walked down the school hallways
And I saw you walking with your friends
My face accidentally hit a locker and closed it
My books dropped
You came up to my books
And picked them up
You handed them to me
I was going to say thank you
But I couldn't manage to say that
I just saw your beautiful eyes looking into mine
And I immediately began to blush
Oh no, I'm blushing in front of a guy
Who's really cute
And has gorgeous eyes
Like a sunset
I….I….I….I
Wanted to say something
But I love you
You're…..you're
Really cute
I finally manage to say, "Thank you," with my
angelic voice
You said, "No problem, wow, you're pretty."
You're blushing
I blush too
I said "I should get to class."
You said "I'll walk you there, what class do you
have."
I said "En, English!"
He said, "May I escort you?"
I said, "Yes, thank you!"
He said "No problem!"

You escorted me to English class
And you gently pulled me aside
You told me, "I love you."
You gave my cheek a kiss
I began to blush
I dropped my books again
I said, "Oops," as I looked at them
He said to me, "It's okay love!"
I love you, I seriously love you.

Lucy told mom recently that she wants to have a boyfriend and kiss him in the basement "like Ceci did." When mom brought this up, _in front of my dad_, I choked on my coffee.

"It's not fair that I can't have a boyfriend because of Down Syndrome."

There have been many friends, family members, strangers, that have brought up the idea of Lucy dating (and marrying!) a boy with Down Syndrome, and how cute and perfect that would be. It's all well intentioned and they've all read an article or seen a video somewhere about a DS couple who fell in love and live happily ever after. But Lucy hates this idea, she's offended by it. That she is reduced to dating someone exactly like her. That she doesn't get a fair chance at love like the rest of us.

This triggers the root of one of Lucy's biggest insecurities: when people limit her just by looking at her.

What mom told me

" Without a Lucy, a world will not be set in
front of her."

The voice that's within me speaks this and is
known by my mom as well. She spoke those words
well and could tell God had made someone he loves
so much more than anything and he's right next to
me (where he has been all along). I'm more than
someone with Down Syndrome and I know that from
the bottom of my heart and my parents and sister.
They love me for who I am and not because of DS.

I'm more than that.

From pain, part 3.

Ivan Sturman died from a heart attack on October 13th 2016.

One week later, my parents, my sister, my nana and I sat around a table at what was their favorite restaurant in El Cerrito, in mostly silence. Barely three month ago, we sat there with him.

It was too hard to make conversation with my parents and my nana who were making an effort to recognize all the friends and family that had kindly reached out to them, so instead I sat solemnly with my sister, who stared blankly at her spaghetti and meatballs. She often did that when we ate with our grandparents.

When Lucy is uncomfortable her body freezes in a haze with her eyebrows furrowed and her eyes wide, she is often staring down at a table or a floor and she remained in this haze through his funeral.

"Jane!" One of my nana's friend's came up to the table. My nana looked startled. "I'm...so sorry for your loss" Her friend began to cry when she acknowledged each one of us at the table. "Oh look, you're all here. Good." When she reached down to pull my mother into a big hug, my mom started to cry too, and like dominos, Lucy and I broke down.

A few minutes later, when the friend left and we went back to eating, my nana began to talk about her gardener, then paused to ask why everyone was crying. I watched Lucy's eyebrows furrow deeper.

Pain flushed through, no matter how desperately it was trying to be shoved down. It flushed with confusion, shame, sorrow, anger, exhaustion. All together. For me at least.

My grandfather led an interesting life, I am told. He was admired by many. Lucy and I just didn't get to see that side of him. I'm glad that my father was able to see him in those ways.

After dessert, my sister and I sat outside on a bench while my parents closed out the bill. She rested her head on me and cried. "I just miss grandma, Ceci".

I put my arm around my sister and pulled her tighter.
I knew.

Bodies

My sister and I — we are writers. We always have been, we always will be.

I would not begin to understand myself as a writer — and, cue, Descartes, I would not begin to understand myself at all, without my sister. I must acknowledge that. I also would not be as empathetic, as patient, as humble, as light, as many other things — but perhaps most importantly, I could not ever feel at home in my own body, my own mind.

When I think about having a creative identity, there is a certain sentiment that I am unable to escape. It is from Helene Cixous in *The Laugh of The Medusa*. I remember first reading this passage when I was doing a research project at the university writing center.

"Censor the body and you censor breath and speech at the same time. Write yourself. Your body must be heard."

That night I went home and journaled about all of the times that I have stifled my own creativity. How I have refused to admit that all I have ever wanted to do, all I have ever felt happy doing, felt completely at peace with myself with is writing. How I have effectively been censoring my body for my entire life by denying myself as a writer.

Lucy on the other hand has lived her life wonderfully unashamed and devoted to being a writer. Lucy claims writing before all else; she understands, more than anyone I know, that her body must be heard. She understands it so deeply and so profoundly.

My sister loves taking risks. She has lived unafraid of societal consequences and failures. She has forced people to know her worth, as created, as a creative, as a creator.

For most of my life and sometimes still I am scared to admit out loud that I am a creative person, because I believe that if I do so, I am committing out loud to be a *talented*, creative person, and I am far too scared of failure or of shame to do so.

But Lucy reminds me that for some reason, we have been hand selected to create,

We have been graced with a balancing act.

Just as her body must be heard, of course my body must be heard.

I am creative.

Lucy has changed how I see myself and my body and my creative identity. We must be heard together.

Create

My sister is right when she says I'm a creative person. She thinks I show so much in writing and I do. She tells me all the time, "This is great, you know you have so much creativity." When she can say something like that, I feel good about myself. At a young age, dancing had created me into being a creative person, and just acting in a Christmas pageant and singing in children's choir made it grow so much. "I have a stiff hand when I do art." As an elementary student, I was very, very artistic in my art class because my mind was so unique in the light I saw from my eyes. I was so into drawing, painting, and water coloring when I was outside of school. I was a middle schooler when I joined chorus and I saw many beams of light in front of my eyes. During my years as a high schooler, I saw many things bloom into a passion full of light and inspiration. That was called theatre. In the writing process for stories, scripts, and poems, my imagination has brought what was I made to be by living in the moment. Creativity is me.

Attention

My parents were convinced that Lucy could grow up
to live a "normal" life if they worked hard
enough. They were encouraged because as Lucy got
older and older, she showed more and more
promise. She started talking earlier and with
more clarity than many other DS kids, she wasn't
tested as mentally retarded, her eye-hand
coordination was almost regular. They joined the
PA Down Syndrome society right away.

By the time my sister was five, she had already
been to more doctors and therapists than most
people will see in their entire lives, each one
offering their own opinion on what could make her
a ~super high functioning Down Syndrome kid~. My
parents decided to immediately enroll her in
speech therapy. They worked with a specialist who
started her off on the drug Synthroid at just one
month old, which would adjust her natural thyroid
levels, keep her body healthy, and enhance her
growth trajectory. She had two eye surgeries
before the age of four: one when they realized
that she had strabismus (double vision) and the
other when they realized she had a blocked tear
duct.

When I was younger, I blamed my parents for all
the attention Lucy got. Ceci hold on. Ceci, not
right now. Ceci, be quiet. Ceci, you're making
your sister upset. It was unfair. And I wished I
was Lucy so I could get that attention too.

Body

This body I have
Has tons of flaws
Some I like
Most of it I don't like
I'm getting used
To it
Since it's unique
I wish I could like
My body
And more things about it
It has changed
Over the years
When I was young
I never thought
This body
Was my favorite part of me
I thought "Ugh, why do I have this?"
But it has changed
And brought many flaws
The worst part
Makes me sick
Which is this nasty and gross
Thing, hurting my hips
Giving me cramps
This is my least favorite
Thing about my body
I'm not trying
To judge the looks
Of my body
These are my opinions
At least that's what I think
I like my shoulders,
The back of my neck,
My right hand, and both of my feet
This body may not be perfect
But that's okay.

Body, cont.

Sometimes I think about what it would be like if Lucy's mind was in my body and vice versa. I think that Lucy - in my body - would be radiant in her confidence, that she would never have to hear a man tell her to smile more, she is beautiful when she smiles, because she would just smile all the time. She would love my body. She would love how it performs something she has never been able to perform. She would worship it. She would somehow make it more beautiful than it has ever been.

And I would wallow in pity and self-hatred.

I wish I could give my body to her, so she could treat it right, so she could love it, more than I ever could.

I think about how I am naturally melancholic and she is naturally radiant and I am so grateful to have her to show me how to be radiant sometimes, to remind me I am radiant.

I love the way my cheeks rise up to my eyelashes when I am turned sideways, how they touch my eyes when I laugh, I love that they are still wide enough to remind me that I am still young, I still have much to learn.

I love that I share my nose with my sister, other than our hair it is the only touchable feature that we share. She reminds me that we have cute noses, small and lifted.

I love my brown eyes, not just in the sun when they are golden, but in the dark, when they dance amongst the shadows.

I love my eyebrows like I love my teeth, because they remind me that I am visible to others, that I am desirable in some regards, they remind me

how nice it feels to be complimented so I must do
it to others, to myself more often. But I love
how my eyebrows feel, too - coarse and wild
against my golden eyes.

My freckles, how they come to decorate me.
My hair, twisted and unruly and free,
My ears, the most sensitive part of me. The most
uncontrolled. How they can chill me

I love my hands because they can create, and they
can create so well. They know how to dance better
than I ever will and they prove to me that looks
and size do not equal worth, nor talent.

I love my arms because they have always been
strong. I have always been pulling myself up. I
will always pull myself up with these arms.

The triangle of my back, it slims along my waist,
but it is tall and hard at its summit. It cracks
when I breathe in and I love that. I love its
promise to me, it is the strongest part of me
despite all that I have put it through, and I
will never even see it.

My legs, I have hated them for so long because of
their unattractiveness but I have recently began
to love the way that my muscles pop and retract,
how they are firm, how much they can stretch, how
much they can hold.

My feet, how fast they can take me, although
sometimes I wish they would take me a bit slower.
How they refuse to drag.

Imperfect

Underneath the makeup
The running down mascara
Smudged lip gloss
Eyeliner all messed up
A beautiful face looking gorgeous
Glows like the sun every morning
Beautiful in the inside and out
Even though there's flaws
The cheeks are pretty like a sunset
Even when they get red
When the face
Is tired from the outside
Or its skin, dry
Your face is perfect
Exactly like you.

Love

Recently, I was driving to the gym, and Lucy was
in the passenger seat with me. It has only been
in the last year or so that Lucy has abandoned
her fear of my driving and started sitting in the
front seat with me.

In the cup-holder between us was a bulletin for
the funeral service that I had attended earlier
that day. I wanted to talk to Lucy about it, so I
asked her if she knew I went to a funeral earlier
that day.

                                               Yes,
she said

Do you know how he died? I asked

        Yes. Suicide. But…I didn't want to ask you
            because I didn't want you to be upset.

Why would I be upset, girl?

She looked down.

I asked her if she knew anyone that thought about
suicide, she said no. I asked her if she knew why
people thought about suicide, she said no.

I thought about what I could say to her. I could
say so much. As I turned into the gym parking
lot, I told her about mental illness, which she
knew about. I told her about how people with an
affinity to mental illness like depression or
anxiety are more likely to have suicidal
thoughts.

I told her about how sometimes terrible things
can happen or a terrible feeling can grow and
grow in your mind, like the terrible feeling when
she thinks that me and mom and dad are mad at her

and she can't function until she is assured she
is forgiven,
and it will all of a sudden trap you, it will
suffocate you, but it does not go away quickly
like when one is assured that their family has
forgiven them, instead it will feel as though you
will never escape that feeling, that you will
never be happy again, that you have no choice but
to end your life to feel happy, all because of
your mind, all because it decides to hurt you.

We stayed in the car

Lucy looked very concerned.

                                        Ceci,
she paused.
   I don't know how to say this but have you ever
                              thought about it?

I looked at her.
Suicide? No, girl.

                  I'm just worried about your anxiety.

Well you don't have to worry about that.
I promise you.

Lucy put her hand on my leg and asked me if she
could pray for me, right then and there. Lucy
asked God to take away my anxiety. She asked God
to tell me he loves me, right then and there, to
not let me listen to lies in my head. She prayed
for my classmate who died.

For two weeks after that, she texted me every
morning to wish me good morning and tell me she
loved me.

Hands

Hands to create.

Inspiration

We were born with the word inspire
We discover it from music and people
We also grew up around it
Inventive
Minds
Inquiring
Genius
Insights
Naturally
Able
To
Inspire
Others
Now
Making dreams for us all the time when we are
asleep
Our hearts shows it as well
It's the best feeling in our generation
For people like us
We make it happen
We show it to the world
Our parents gave it us
And we stand on it
In the world we were blessed with
God gave it all of us
And we spread inspiration
To anyone who needs it...

Hope is the word
That helps me to think of it
People tell me I'm that person to them
People and music and hope builds it for me
My sister does that too
I'm more than just someone
Who's behind the feeling of being alone
I set myself to believe in it
I see it shine everywhere I am
I'm raised on the word
And know what it means to people.

Whenever something inspires you

Enabled

You feel inspired
And there are no words to say anything
Because your heart is in it too
It's a feeling you love, love, love the most in
the entire world
God has made it for you
Your parents have
Friends too
Everyone else as well
Inspiration is the word to come to
Even when you're stuck
Especially in writing when you need your mind to
wrap in it
A perfect thing in life to need
Call inspiration when you need it the most in the
world.

Inspiration, cont.

Do you know what it feels like when the universe
desires something of you?

it denies to pass you by like it does with the
others,
or perhaps it denies you the ability to opt out
of it —
it welcomes itself in gently, slowly, privately,
it compliments you well and most of the time it
just feels like

that first moment a sliver of sunlight escapes
from the clouds
to draw up your face to the ocean, to rest its
lips on your eyelids and remind you of your own
warmth,
for a while it is just like that
for a while it doesn't mind that you use it for a
high, a fix, every so often when you are bored
and cold,
for a while it is hopelessly devoted to waiting
for you because it knows that when the time comes
for you to choose it or to not,

that it feels too good for you to not
and whether you know it or not it is woven itself
so deeply into your organs that you will not know
how to not
even though you desire to know how to not,
or to feel autonomous, even though if you felt
autonomous you wouldn't feel as important,
as though the universe desires something out of
you.

you are fearful to choose it.
not because you don't believe in your own warmth,
because you know how patient it has been with you
after all you have put it through,
after how long you have used it.

and because you don't yet know how to become even
warmer,

you don't believe that when you begin to be
patient with it, after all these years,
because you have just discovered you must,
you don't believe it will continue to be patient
with you.

it will, you tell the both of you, it must
you must, it tells you, you will.

Dreams, reality

I have a feeling
Inside of me, which is
Feeling like a monster
I feel uncomfortable in my own skin
On the outside of me
I get so embarrassed of myself
I hate this feeling
I want to get rid of it
I don't want to feel like a monster
Whenever I am.

I feel inspired
By music,
By books,
By my friends,
And my parents
I love the word inspire
It makes me feel
Calm and it opens
My imagination, my creative imagination
I feel I'm just me.

There's one thing
I can't stop thinking about
Which is my grandma Delsie
I love her
She's the person
With welcome arms
I miss her
She's everything to me
I think about her
All the time
I'm thankful she's in my life.

All of my dreams
Are mostly craziness
And nightmares
Just a little bit of happy dreams
They're fading from my mind
I feel like I'm not having
Any good dreams

This isn't great
Where are my happy dreams
Where are they right now
I'm not thinking straight
In my sleep
I feel that my mind
Is not creative
Anymore, anymore.

My body is changing
I'm growing up
I feel like I'm an adult
I'm a new me
I do adult things (well, as an adult student)
This is me now
I am no longer a baby anymore.

My talents make
Me creative
I put my imagination first
I let it make me travel
In new places
When I dance
I feel comfortable in my skin
When I write
I use all of my thinking
When I was and used
To be a part of RRPA
I felt I was in a better place
I belonged to.

I never daydreamed
I like being in reality
I do imagine
I keep my dreams real
I mean what I say
Being real is just me
I'm saying on my behalf
I like reality.

Never had stopped
Trying to believe
My dreams are real

I made them real for myself
One of them was
Graduating high school
I accomplished that dream
But that was one of
The dreams I had on my mind
I still have the ones
I'm not desperate for
But want them in my life
I'm desperate to become an author
My dreams are
Real, very real.

Best time of my life
Was when I came into my sister's life
She has become the person
Who can always support me
She gave me so much love
She showed an act of love
I was a baby
When she held me
She smiled showing
That she loved me
She's so cute
Cute, cute baby
Thinking about
Making a connection
As sisters with me
Will be exciting.

As a Junior
In high school
I took a bus
To NYC
To see my sister
I went by myself
Doing something brave
I felt I did fine
I was doing great
I was proud of myself
Right now
I'm going to NYC
To see my sister

Enabled

            I'm excited
      This is my third time
   Taking the bus by myself
      I'm an official adult

Mush

I am mush, for my little lamb, I am mush,
her laugh
I am mush

My sister and I got these white fluffy matching
robes for Christmas
and we wear them as we lie together and laugh

Lamb, she calls me,
and I her

Usually she does not prefer to cuddle (I do
because I am mush)
but sometimes I bribe her, and she concedes,
and sometimes,
when she initiates
when she comes into my bed without any prodding
just because she wants to,
I am mush

The way you look at each other is precious,
we are often told
after we are joking and laughing, and then as we
are winding ourselves down my little lamb makes a
humming sound and wraps her arms around me or
lays in my lap

and I am mush.

We were made for each other, I know it, I am
fuller with her.

Sometimes, often,

I allow myself to get scared about how full I am
with her because — what if something were to
happen to her? How could I bear to live without
her? With the sadness of knowing her? How can I
love something so much and trust it to survive
forever?

I think about this often, I am ashamed to admit.

It is because I am so scared of how full she
makes me. I think that my lamb is the most
special lamb to have ever been created and I
don't deserve her and one day God will realize
that and I will be usurped by a more deserving
holder of her love.

But then I think that he loves me so much to give
me this lamb, he loves me as much as I love this
lamb, even more, and
I am mush.

Mush, cont.

Whenever Ceci ends a conversation on a call, she asks me to pray to God for her (which I totally do). I wish she didn't have anxiety, because I want her to feel okay. I love Ceci very much, I know God's watching over her and knows how she feels when anxiety gets in the way. The look on my face when she mentions this to me is very, very worried, and I feel like my eyes are just getting filled up with tears. I can understand how she feels and I can empathize with her. Ceci very easily opens up about her feelings and keeps herself strong. She's relatable. I can relate to her and her feelings. I know she has strength in her, because that's how God created her to be.

Flatland

a few hours ago, I came across the flatland.

vast and emptied with rose colored sand I
wondered how it would look in a different hour

spilt over to the sea, it seeps and it flows
until there is enough of it

so profoundly desolate about the silence

so hollowed yet not at all; if a hole were not a
hole this would be it.

and here I was believing that I would be
filled with what nostalgia empties you of. and
here I was. empty and

hundreds of miles from where I am now and
hundreds more from where I was.

to the right:

when you were young, you flew to another
land. you did not feel fear when the small plane
twisted and turned and all 12 passengers looked
around in nervous anticipation. youth.

you sat in the back of a pickup truck to gather
cement.

you stood to watch the truck drive down and down
into a river, well it must have been a river at
some point. but now trucks drive down into it and
it is filled with old car parts and garbage. a
small layer of grey water covers the ground, the
quiet kind of layer that covers your toes when
the tide rolls in but does not hold any force.

what is most remarkable is the sky, it is not the
same sky as the sky in the town. It is much

larger and much greyer now. It has usurped the
noise of the town and replaced it with nothing.

with or without water you cannot ever imagine
this being a river you would like to go to.

there is no place as vast as this
abandoned river.

you stand outside the truck and you shovel small
rocks in. beside you, women with buckets are
bathing naked and bathing their naked children.
you are frightened to look over because you are
frightened for these women.

you must throw your weight back with every
shovel. and you must throw your eyes back.

you do not want to look at the man watching you
shovel because you do not want to see if he is
watching the naked women.

after you finish and as the truck drives away you
sit in the front and you do not speak as you
watch the sky become the sky again.

to the left:

when you were even younger, you played and
played on a rocky beach with your sister. for
hours, you two made those rocks your home. you
built two story condominiums and gardens outside
of them, you built secret hallways in between
your condominiums. for days you did this. for
summers.

you loved these rocks because they were
many, they were vast and they did not end. and
you made a home in them, of course.

when it was time to eat, you made birthday
cakes out of the rocks for the both of you. and
when you were forced to, you would run to the

blanket where your parents sat on and eat peanut
butter and jelly sandwiches.

         you guys have become very dusty. your mom
would tell you. go clean yourself off in the
water.

         we don't want to. it's cold.

         oh come on.

if your parents took you to a sandy beach with
warm water you maybe your sister would not go on
to have a rock collection and maybe you would not
go on to write fantastically about rocks. but
maybe you (both) would.

         it comes to me slowly and then all at
once.

converging together are my past lives

in the flatland I create.
I sit with my sister at the bottom of the empty
river. we are bathing and as we drive away we
laugh. We lay on our rocks on the back of the
truck and we stare at the grey sky.

What is a disability?

Two voices made this piece come together, but one voice came up with all of it. The voice behind the words up above is my voice.

How I see it, from my parents point-of-view, is that their second daughter is more different than their first-born child.

They were devastated when the doctors broke the news.

Here's the breakdown of a time: I came to my parents to talk about something important and they gave me answers I wasn't expecting to hear.

I cried so, so hard.

I remember hearing one of my parents say, "If you weren't a Lucy, we would be so sad."

I thought in that moment, there had to be a way to cure "my thing" and there wasn't.

NOTHING AT ALL.

I've spent a lot of time around people with Down Syndrome. By no means am I an expert in any way, but I have made some observations.

I have never met a person with Down Syndrome I wouldn't want to hang out with.

They are wonderful people. Sweet, playful, funny, affectionate, full of joy. And this isn't to say they're permanently happy - they experience a wide range of emotions, just like the rest of us. My sister certainly does. The argument that people with Down Syndrome are always happy because they don't realize they have Down Syndrome is so far from true that I don't even want to engage with it.

Lucy can't hold on to anger, nor bitterness, nor jealousy. She has no vindictive bone in her body; she will never hold a grudge. If she feels anger (or bitterness, etc.) she will feel it for a moment, then love and forgiveness will overwhelm her and she will let it go. I can't even put a number to how many times Lucy and I have fought over something stupid and I will storm off and a couple of minutes later she will come knocking at my door, apologizing, asking for my forgiveness, and telling me she loves me.

When I was in the wrong.
I don't deserve this love.

My mom has brought up this idea that perhaps God created us all to be more like Lucy in our unconditional love and forgiveness and joy, and we are indeed disabled in our anger, our bitterness, our jealousy, our anger, etc.

So what is a disability anyways? It surely can't be within the handicapped or non-handicapped binary. That's insultingly simple.

I am many ways that I wish I wasn't. Like Lucy, I have more or less accepted myself, but I still wish I could be a different way.

I am so jealous of Lucy's spirit. I am jealous that if I was Lucy, I wouldn't even be jealous.

If my jealousy and anger and self-doubt and anxiety didn't cripple me and disable me, how would I be enabled?

My sister launched me up onto a pedestal that I never asked to be on. It took me a while to feel comfortable being on that pedestal, and to understand what it even means to be up here. But I'm here now, and I have no option to step down. I do have the option to be very aware of how I am able.

What is a disability?

I had no idea about "my thing" when I was young,
I knew nothing about it. I was with my parents at
one time and we did ASL together. People looked
at me like something was wrong with me, like
"What's wrong with her". There was a time Ceci
was with me. Two young boys were staring at me
and she yelled at them and they ran away. I said
something to her. Another time was when I was at
Chick-Fil-A and a kid looked at me in the
playroom. My mom and Ceci looked at the kid to
make them stop looking at me. "Just look at her".

There's nothing wrong with little kids looking at
me. I just feel like I can't do anything to stop
it from happening. It just happens. More than
once. I remember the times when one kid would do
it, another repeating the process. I don't know
what to do, I really don't. None of that is my
fault, it's their fault, their parents didn't
raise them right. That's what I think.

"Without a learning challenge", that would be
nice. For once I would like to be normal and have
a life that's better and not challenging. But
guess what, that's not going to happen. I'm not
having that life, I want that life and live in
this one. As I think about it, there won't be a
me at all in the world. How will someone as her
be creative, friendly, and caring, if she's not
there. "And without a Lucy, a world would not be
there for her."

I am more than someone who has Down Syndrome (my
thing). "There's many things I am and what I do
best at." I love who I am and I'm proud to be
different (I try my best to understand this is
how God made me and not how I made myself). "I'm
not giving up or stopping myself from everything
in life," I tell myself all the time, "If you
give up, you'll go nowhere" and, "Stopping
yourself from everything in life, your dreams

will be nothing worth of reaching for". As I think about that, it's true (I mean how will you come to a point in life you have to do something and do nothing at all).

"I can be a challenge at times and get into messes all along the way", "But I try to be strong and move past them", and "I may not be perfect and that's okay" All along in my life, I think too much that I want to be perfect living in a perfect world. Being a challenge in the world is not that bad and think it's a good thing (yes, it has ups and sideways and down times), but once you realize for yourself "I need to be strong and move past them." I realize that for myself too. Perfect is a such strong word to speak on when there's nothing to say. It can do nothing as long you can be you. Be strong. It's good to feel like this.

I learned so much from my mom: normal will take away the you in the world. But, if I was normal, and "There won't be a Lucy", I know for me that life will come with little time instead of fast time. I want my life how I want it, but I need to wait when God calls and I can be on the path where I want to follow. Waiting is not a thing for me, I need patience (not impatience).

In the world you realize that what's done is done, you get the experience you have felt throughout your life, and you can't turn back to fix it. God the almighty made you and your life, and the only thing you need to do is what God wants you to do.

Ten Things That Are Different Because of Down Syndrome

1. I have the ability to inspire people
2. I fidget more than others
3. People tend to stare at me more than they need to
4. It takes me a long time to focus
5. I talk in different octaves
6. I can't drive, like others can
7. I have to live with my parents rather than being independent
8. I drink with my tongue sticking out
9. I need to have boundaries, like around food
10. I have to do a lot of advocacy for myself

Ten things that are different because of Down Syndrome, cont.

1. I am softer
2. I am a caretaker, I always will be
3. I grew up faster because of that
4. I understand equity better
5. I understand fairness not at all
6. I can decide if a person is a good person within seconds of their first interaction with my sister
7. I have immense love for people with developmental challenges, I am my kindest around them
8. I wake up every morning with a worth that has been countlessly reminded to me by my sister
9. I pursue work in advocacy and activism
10. I have an infallible source of joy. at my fingertips and forever.

Us

Sisters are the most powerful thing in life. I am blessed I have one. Ceci and I will always be writers and it's our passion. We have valued each other's writings. Ceci shows passion and creativity. I show creativity and life. We are proud to be the people we are today. I learned there's more in life to believe in. To find the passion I was given the gift of. Ceci's gift is helping people to feel like they belong in the world, that matters to me too. Our steps together are making us feel like the world needs to see what it feels like to be empowered people. We want to help people move forward because we have the feeling they need to be heard and be inspired as much as they can. As sisters together, we are a team doing something we care about: helping people.

                              Have you thought about
                     How your future will be and
                        Look like once it comes?
                           You think to yourself
                          When will that happen
                          What do I want to do?
              How would my choices takes me to that place in
                                 the next five years?
             All of that stuff is a decision and risk you're
                        making for yourself in person.

I sit and I sift through pains and I feel the
knots and I know I cannot begin to untangle them
but I can feel them and know them by heart as
they know mine so well and I sift and I feel
knots and I let thoughts come and go knowing so
well that when it is time they will be released
in perfect order and my hands are just the
conduit and my brain can do nothing except for
sift and feel knots and
avoid holes
that are gaping, just avoid, just scale around
and reject to see the crater because you've
already come so far, today, you've already come
so, so far, just take a break. Go back down you
can go to the hole another day it will still be
there I promise you.
And you sit and you think what will I write about
today what have I been harboring what is it time
to release and you think about your heart in the
past couple months and all that you have put it
through with all that sifting and all those knots
and you wonder whether all of that can fit into
something that someone would want to hear or if
it is just for you or if it is for both. You
think about how you don't think about things the
way you used to when you used to think about
things so much and feel so little. You think
about sadness and how you've welcomed him in and
how you've watched him go just from thinking
about him so much and you wonder if you have the
power to do that again, this new you. You think

that you are impressed with yourself now, that
you've started surprising yourself and you are so
thankful that you are not permanently cyclical.
You think about happiness and you know her now.
You think that people can change. You think about
all that you can do and you think you can do it.
You are softer now because of pain, you are
kinder. You laugh out loud when you are alone.
You are sitting in a quiet glass room and you cry
because you feel your own greatness, for the
first time. You cry because you are different and
you are grateful, you cry because you are greater
than your disease for the first time and you are
powerful and you can hear you name and be proud
of it and you can be at peace and because you are
so beautiful and you're going to start
remembering that. You are different now and you
feel the knots so you can know them so well
because they are yours. You will begin to forgive
them and as you are letting this all out you
realize you have begun to love yourself so much
it chokes you up and you can't even look at the
words as they come out you must look at the
cities passing by the ones you will be able to
love yourself in, and you are crying now because
when you have only hated yourself for so long and
when you have only hurt yourself no matter how
much you are loved by those who love you there is
no better feeling than to be freed.

I plan for my future
I know who I want to be
How will my dreams come true
I do know I need to take some time
I do know that
Whatever I come up with
I need to show it and not through words and
pictures, but with proof that I want it.

Independence

I get excited
About an adventure
When I travel
I also get happy
Knowing I'm going to have fun
And have good food for my body
I get to relax
And kick back with my feet up
Happy, happy me
I'm feeling calm
Sun's up
Moon's up when the sun goes down
I'm having fun for myself
There's the beach
And amazing things to do
I think I'm just lucky
With a smile on my face
Showing how much I'm enjoying myself
Yay, yay, and yay
For me to feel this happy
The best, best part of traveling
Is sightseeing, the scenery of the sights
Are just so beautiful to look at
I love seeing it
It makes me happy in the inside and outside
They're pretty up close
Amazing too
So, so incredibly beautiful
The food makes me happy
And makes my stomach happy too
It looks super yummy in front of me
It thinks about getting into my stomach
Saying "Hey, we need you, we seriously need you."
I just love to travel.

Independence, cont.

A few years back, my sister visited me in New York, by herself for the first time. She took a bus from Union Station in D.C. to Port Authority Bus Terminal in NYC. I was on the F train from Queens, where I lived at the time, when the subway stopped. Not unusual. Would honestly be unusual if it didn't stop. But soon I realized this wasn't a typical delay, and when 20 minutes passed without moving, I started to panic. I accounted for some lee-way, but not that much. If the train didn't move, I wouldn't be able to pick Lucy up in time from the bus stop. And for the next ten minutes, I sat, frozen, catastrophically thinking about all of the terrible things that would happen to my 16 year old sister with Down Syndrome when she got off of the bus and no one was there to pick her up. Of course, I had no service underground to text her or call her. I searched around for panicked looks on my fellow passengers' faces to fuel my anxiety even further. Finally, we started to move - just at the time Lucy's bus was scheduled to arrive. The conductor announced that there had been an accident, a "sick passenger", and someone in my train murmured that a "homeless person probably died again". I felt a pang of pain in my chest - guilt now for feeling angry at the delays coupled with my existing anxiety about abandoning Lucy. I arrived to her bus drop-off location 25 minutes late, tears welling and chest pounding. I saw that there was no bus.

I called her and she told me she was at a café. I found her at this café, chatting with a young woman from her bus, the woman she'd sat next to who was kind enough to not leave her alone when she got off the bus and her flakey sister was M.I.A. I ran up to her and hugged her. I'm so sorry Lucy. I'm so sorry. She laughed me off.

It's totally fine, Cec, don't worry at all. This is my friend Beck!

Hi, thank you so much, I shamefully thanked the woman, not even able to look her in the eyes.

It's no problem at all. Your sister is awesome, she smiled at me. I know, I smiled back.

Later, we found out that Beck worked at the White House. Not only that, she was President Obama's stenographer. Her kindness extended to staying in touch, eventually sending Lucy a high school graduation present and even offering my family a tour of the White House.

When my parents found out about this, they were fuming. I don't think any of us accurately estimated Lucy's ability to figure it out without the rest of us. But if I know anything now, she can get through life solely by charming the socks off of strangers.

The rest of the weekend, we ate and laughed our way through NYC. She invited all my friends over to my dorm room for a dance party at 10 pm, then conked out in my bed at 8pm. She loves to tell the story now, of how she conquered the city by herself.

When we surprised ourselves

I never knew I could do Partners in Policymaking,
I mean the experience was so powerful.

In summer of 2016, I was invited to a week-long
seminar for people with disabilities to learn
about advocacy. It was called Youth Leadership
Forum. I went to Petersburg, Virginia, all by
myself. I was on VSU campus. I was shy at first,
which is unusual because I'm an extrovert. It was
the first time I left home to do something like
this. I never traveled without my parents or my
sister. This seminar was about becoming mature,
true to yourself, and learn about how to make a
difference for people who have disabilities. It
was scary at first but eventually I liked it.

I met a friend who lives close to me (she was an
introvert). She was the most well-spoken person
I've ever met who has a disability. She and I
became the best of friends.

Because of YLF, I was invited to do PIP. Partners
in Policymaking is an advocacy group in Richmond,
Virginia, with Virginia Board of People with
Disabilities. I was invited to be on the team,
and I was the only person with a disability to be
there. Also, I was the only young adult with only
other adults - moms and dads. Once a month I
traveled to Richmond to attend meetings and meet
with legislators to speak about how to educate
students with disabilities in schools and
change's the school districts' minds about
disabilities. And make sure they are including
people with disabilities in regular classes with
their friends, not just self-contained classes,
being bored.

When I was in those self-contained classes in
High School, I felt like I wasn't being included
and my parents and I had to fight hard in IEP
meetings for me to be with all my friends. My

case manager thought it was too much for me but I thought it wasn't too much for me. I wanted to be just like my friends and have a normal high school experience.

It was a big deal to be a part of PIP. Leaving my house to go to Richmond every month was the most amazing thing my parents had ever seen me do. I felt included. Since I like traveling, I knew it was different but I wanted to make Ceci proud of me.

Being inspired by Ceci motivated me to advocate for people because she and I always had our talks. Sisterly talks.

When we surprised ourselves, cont.

It was a risk, this day I gave myself in Phoenix
and it was an accident too, a
stupid overlook of a conference schedule.
Normally, I don't like to give myself days like
this;
days empty and excess, full of nothing but myself

I was anxious about this day in Phoenix
Even though I, for the past four or so years,
have been convinced I am naming my first child
after the city,
albeit
never going farther south than Virginia
absent of Florida, a couple, tragic times,
New Orleans

but Phoenix was the desert, I thought

And my mind loves to remind me of the desert I
was in for 6 weeks
in my own mind, in my own space,
fourteen air hours away
alone in a town with much different skin
unwelcomed and locked up in an apartment where I
was told I must stay, it was safe there for me
and I was
hurting from being alone
hurting when I called my family and was reminded
of how alone I was
hurting because I couldn't tell anyone around me
about what my mind was doing to me for six weeks
because there were more important tasks at hand
hurting
and scared

I thought, I will be in Phoenix and I will hurt
again with the excess day
and I will have
nothing to do but think about what my mind does
to me.

I will be in the desert,
but I am a city girl, lifted up by strangers
working next to me in neighborhood coffee shops
that are probably lonely like me, if I asked

And I thought about this day so much that when
people asked me about Phoenix my stomach hurt
because I knew it would be the worst mistake of
my life to give myself an extra day in Phoenix.
Traveling alone is not for me, no

Since I was fourteen air hours away, I don't give
myself excess days in deserts, I don't even give
myself excess hours in my city, I give myself
excess of efficiency and I fill up my mind with
all of the things to do and I fear for when I
have nothing to do and then I must sit and wait,
for what is waiting for me.

And sometimes I fear so powerfully that I cannot
be efficient and then I am mad at myself but I am
still scared,
I am so scared of emptiness
I don't want to breathe that freely.

I only have me and
I don't want her right now
so I avoid her in excess days in Phoenix

I woke up early because of the time change and I
thought to myself, I can't go back to sleep
so I found a path nearby to run
and I ran along the Arizona canal for miles until
I got to a golf course,
which was beautiful so I stopped to take a
picture
and then I ran back.
And the whole time I was breathing in a different
way without humidity and I was running faster and
longer and I was proud of myself and it was much
more beautiful than my usual run where I must
cross many dirty streets to get to a park not
nearly as beautiful as this.

And then I found a town and I found a place for
juice and a bagel and the barista smiled at me,
he probably likes me, I thought, then I realized
he probably doesn't like me I'm just not used to
smiling.

And then I went back to my hotel and I ate the
bagel outside and felt the warm, but not too hot,
sun, welcoming me in, and I went upstairs and I
took a bath and I shaved my legs for the first
time in probably three months
and I laid in my bed and fell asleep again.
And then I woke up and I went back to the town
and I went to a local coffee shop and this
barista smiled at me too.
And I bought myself an iced almond latte and a
vegan apricot oatmeal cookie that I devoured in
about three seconds, then I applied for a
research trip to Bangladesh because I don't
learn, then I called my dad and listened to him
talk about what he was anxious about and felt so
touched that he would be so vulnerable with me,
and I felt so understood and so much love, and
then I walked around the town and went into
different shops and found some essential oils and
soap made locally with healing powers and I
thought I need to be healed so I bought a lot of
them which is something I would never usually do.

And then I went back to the hotel and my friend
Sheetal called me and said do you want to go for
a hike with me and I said yes I would love to
Sheetal and then she picked me up and we drove to
Camelback mountain and we scaled up beautiful
rocks and I felt happy to be scaling rocks and
have good health and I thought about:
       fourteen air hours away when my family
       came and saved me and we went up a
       mountain for seven days and scaled up
       so many rocks and my hourly snack
       breaks and my Swahili lessons every
       night and how small my bladder was and
       how often I peed on the side of

mountain and when I thought I was
going to die for sure but instead my
dad and I reached the top and cried
together.
And then Sheetal and I laughed together and were
real people together in Phoenix and we trashed
our home, New York City, together when we saw how
beautiful this desert was, and how happy it made
us to drive and feel in awe.

And I smiled about the red clay and how much it
soothed me and how much the mountains comforted
me and how crisp the air was for me to breathe
in.

And then she dropped me off and I went back to
the hotel and then I wanted Mexican food. The
best I'd ever had, so I looked up Mexican food
with vegan options and I found one 0.4 miles away
and so I took my Malcolm Gladwell book and I
walked over, thinking to myself, I am going to
eat at a restaurant by myself for the first time
in a while. It's going to be nice to focus on my
food and not have to feel self-conscious about
how fast I eat my food in the company of others.
I got to the restaurant and the girl was so nice
to me, and she brought me chips as I ordered a
blackberry mojito:
I don't normally order drinks with
dinner, but I was in the habit since
my coworkers kept buying me drinks and
dinner, probably because they felt bad
because my company doesn't pay interns
even though it's a human rights
organization and I didn't really care
regardless because I keep getting free
drinks and dinner and a trip to
Phoenix and to work with some of the
most important people in New York
City, in my opinion,
and started reading my book. And I read but then
I started listening to the men at the table next
to me talking about work and life, and thinking,

surprised, I don't hate their conversation, these
are nice guys. Then I ordered my vegetable fajita
with beans and fried potatoes on the side and
started messaging my family and my best friend
about how much I love Phoenix and how happy it
makes me and we should all go. After I finished I
went back to the hotel and I got myself a free
trial of hulu so that I could watch Handmaids
Tale and think damn Elizabeth Moss are you
really, actually, a scientologist?

I go to brush my teeth and I think about all of
the times for six weeks that I would brush my
teeth and then turn all of the lights off for
myself,
because no one else would,
The nights I would
sit alone at restaurants and read and then
eavesdrop on my neighbors' conversations, or if I
couldn't understand, eavesdrop on their body
language,
The mornings I would
wake up to write with god
then
walk myself over to the gym to run
and then
breathe crisp air,
How I forced myself to like myself,
to have fun with myself,
and how I did, actually.

How it got harder when I went back to my city and
I felt different and detached and floating and
then I got
              early onset post-traumatic stress
       disorder, my therapist thought, because I
       was forced to think about the scary things
       I wouldn't allow myself to think about when
       I was alone and
because I still think about my future in that
way.

A day in Phoenix was empty and it was healing

I think to others,
I appear hard and strong, but my hardness is as
thin as eggshells that are basically irrelevant
to me anymore (see: vegan apricot oatmeal scone)
but for the sake of the metaphor, I am easily
breakable and very soft and mushy and I feel like
I am more sensitive than anyone I know

to myself,
I feel too incapable of leading myself out of
darkness but I am actually harder than I think
and I am stronger and I am able to be happy and
not scared which is basically what I want more
than anything, I think.

In Phoenix I could breathe,
and do it freely
I wasn't scared anymore.

And I think I can give myself another excess day
I can give myself a couple of them,
I can travel and I can stay at home and I can be
with myself.

I will be scared but not forever, I think
It can come and it can go and I can let it go
more than I think I can
I think.

Mountains

KILIMANJARO, TZ, JULY 2017

In the summer of 2017 I led a research project in Kigoma, Tanzania - assessing gaps and opportunities for aid in three different refugee camps. We planned for my family to join me at the end, and the moment when my parents and sister touched down in that small dimly lit airport - the kind where you can drive up to the runway and hop on your plane, maybe have a quick pat down before you walk up the stairs and find your seat - I felt a massive, visceral euphoria that filled every ounce of my depletion. It lasted for the three and a half weeks until I flew back to New York alone.

When they arrived I exhaled for the first time in a month. And I cried, I didn't have to hold my tears back. I wished I was the same girl I was the last time they saw me a month prior.

I think sometimes you must learn hard things about yourself and you cannot do it where you are comfortable. Not even a little bit comfortable. You need to be stripped of familiar faces and time zones and languages and you need to be on your own. You will be better because of it, you will understand people better and you will be kinder because of it.

We did not have to talk about what I'd seen, we could if I wanted to, but I didn't want to.

Sometimes I'd let it out in small pieces and talk about the children I watched, dusted with red dirt and without shoes, how they couldn't go to school or the women, looking in my eyes me telling me how they'd get assaulted when they lined up for water at early hours of the morning, my security guard who made me nervous and never left my side.

The next day, my mother, father, sister and I

began our climb of Mount Kilimanjaro — one of the
highest mountains in the world.

And me, I often thought about how I was doing
physically the hardest thing I've ever done
immediately after I did emotionally the hardest
thing I've ever done. And me, I could not even
forgive myself for being so traumatized when I
wasn't even experiencing the trauma firsthand.

My family.
We knew this trip would either make or break us
as a collective. Seven uninterrupted days of only
each other — climbing together, eating together,
sleeping in cramped tents together. Of course we
had the help of the mountain guides, strong local
men, sometimes they were just boys, that led us
and carried most of our weight. And I tried to
learn Swahili to keep my mind busy and have an
escape but for the most part we only could spoke
to each other.

We made it.
Of course bickered and we grew impatient with
each other (I will take the blame for the
majority of that) but for the most part, we were
stronger than we have ever been, more in love
than we have ever been. We were in this together.

Each day, we would wake up at seven to climb. And
we climbed for the majority of the day, growing
higher and colder. Our legs hardening and
tightening and tiring. We walked through forests
and deserts and rock formations and craters.

Each night, Lucy and I would snuggle close to
each other and laugh about the silly things that
happened that day. The food dad spilled down his
chest, the way mom mispronounced thank you in
Swahili, how much we would give for an avocado.

We laughed about our dreams. Malaria medicine
made us have crazy dreams and we would compare

who's was sillier. Lucy always had the silliest —

> Winning a talent show and then mom showing
> up and giving her hot dogs —eating bugs—
> going to Hogwarts

We recorded a video diary that we could always
look back on and laugh.

Often my parents would yell from their tent over
for us to be quiet and we would laugh even more.

I am younger, with my sister.

On the hikes, my sister and I preferred to stick
together. We naturally walked at different paces
but I preferred to hold her hand and guide her
down slippery terrains and she preferred to hold
mine over any other hands.

I preferred how she kept me safe from my pain.

Just like when we were younger, I would guide
Lucy across the rocks of Rockport or I would walk
her across the street or I would walk her through
an airport. Even when I could trust her to walk
herself I still preferred to hold her hand.

Lucy would fall asleep early and I would lay and
listen to her quiet breaths and stare up at the
ceiling of the tent until I too fell asleep.

Mountain of more than five thousand feet
Steep slopes and cliffs all around
Rocks were spread out everywhere
Some paths were easy
Most of them were hard
And tiring
I held on the trees to lift me up
Including my balance
The sun was shining
Perfectly in the beautiful blue sky
Gleaming so well
It blended into the day
When it went down
The night was cool
But muggy
And extra, extra cool
The other mornings
Was hard
I took my time
To lean in and trust
In my climbing
I kept going and going
I thought I can do that
I rock climbed
Some of it was easy
Most of it was just fine
Since I struggled
A-lot, I felt like falling
But I trusted myself
Of how I was proud of myself
I kept going
Instead of stopping in my tracks
I did that a couple of times
To catch my breath
Hearing my heartbeat
Drink water for hydration
And to cool off on the way down
There was mud, tons of mud because of the rain
The air felt so muggy
There were cracks between the floor beds
It was very slippery
But it wasn't bad
Only good and amazing.

The morning of the final ascent I woke up to my fathers' nudge. "It's time," he smiled at me. "Good morning," We laughed. The morning was actually 11pm.

I rolled over and put as many layers as I could on while still in my sleeping bag and repeated the ascent mantra--.

When we began, only flashlights led the way. The goal was to catch the sunrise at the top, seven hours later.

--pole, pole, slowly, slowly

--you are not racing anyone

--you will think you are going a bit crazy but it is just the mountain. Just one step in front of another—

The higher we got, the harder it got.

I walked one step behind my father and we inched forward, barely lifting our feet off the ground as we zig zagged up the incline in big Eskimo suits. Sometimes we would pass fellow hikers sitting on the side of the mountain, vomiting - it would take everything within me not to join them.

All of my water bottles froze and so I had to drink from the guides' bottles. But I didn't want to drink anything at all, take my goggles and ski mask off, open my mouth and expose it to cool liquid. You will have to remember to expend as little energy as you possible can, the guides told us in preparation.

As the altitude sharply inclined (we were already starting at 15,000 feet and we picked up 4,000 more), I absolutely did feel like I was going crazy.

Step.

Step.

Step.

Step.

Right.

Left.

Right.

Steps were so monotonous and detached from the rest of my body. My head spun faster and I became dizzier and dizzier but I could not open my mouth so I would have conversations with my father and the guides in my head. *There is no view worth this*, I screamed and no one flinched.

You will find it personally oppressive, someone told me about the ascent.

Three or four hours in, I decided I could not go further, I felt nauseous and I could not keep my balance. I hunched over and dry heaved as the guides and my father watched me. My guide Peter told me that I was fine, that I must keep going.

I am not fine, I mumbled. When I die, you'll see.

It was that bad.

Every few minutes, like a child in the backseat, I would ask how much longer we had. Not long, they told me, not long.

Yeah right, I groaned. These people, forcing me to my death.

At one point, I could not stand straight. I could not take a step without tilting backwards so one guide stood behind me for the rest of the trip to keep me straight.

My father later told me that he was worried about me but he could not even open his mouth to do anything about it.

You are here, Peter told us, you made it.

He paused, just up this last hill to the top.

This last hill looked like an entire extra mountain, like baby Kilimanjaro on top of regular Kilimanjaro.

You are kidding me. I cannot go forward one more step. My dad and I looked at each other. I tried to laugh but I just collapsed to the ground and dry heaved.

When I was in the refugee camps, not too far away:

I know how to be brought low and I know how to abound

I know how to exist in large numbers
I know how to exist in none at all

I know how to cry out to the mercy of any that might hear me
I know how to mute them

I know how to mask myself in strength and dignity
to become these things, even.
yet
I know how to shatter the masks out of utter contempt

and I don't know how to exist in between facade and pain

I know how to feel nothing and everything at once
to desire to feel nothing and everything at once
I know how to not feel
to feel
not

I know how to feel as though my own skin detains me
my own mind disables me
I know how to chew myself up, to spit myself out
to desire myself
to feel myself go

I know how to feel the comfort of my mother, my love, my country, my home
and sometimes, well, most times,
I wish I didn't know how to

yet, I know it all,
I know
I know

When we finally reached the top, UHURU point, the first thing I did was tell my father there is no (insert expletive here) way we are going any further to the "real hiker view point" that "is the actual top" 30 minutes further. Right here is good, great. Perfectly great. I feel real here. He laughed and I laughed and we both cried and held each other as we looked out, at what we did.

Slowly

It will stick to your throat and at first, you
will wonder
    Politely
How long it desires to take.

    Fiery, but it won't burn,
    Fiery but you still taste the salt, that
feels oh, so familiar
So that is why you will only wonder politely, for
now

      In years you will back on it:
    The fire,
And you will not think it so

Slowly,
    The stick will still not burn
    And the fire will still be
    And the salt will still taste, only it is
not so familiar anymore,
    Instead it reminds you of itself in a
different time, when it was more familiar,
    A time that was kinder to your throat even
if it was
    Harsher to it
So you will decide that you don't want to be so
polite anymore, you will have to decide it.

In the summers when you were young, you would
pass by a store that made saltwater taffy, you
would stop and stare through the window at the
heavy rolls of it, blue and pink and, your
favorite, emerald green.
You would watch the rolls slowly twist and turn
into themselves:
       form themselves, and then destroy
       themselves, and then form themselves
       again.
It brought you a sweet sadness and

now that you have grown to despise the way
it sticks to your teeth, you will still upon
occasion remember how it formed
    and wonder, if
slowly,
    you have begun to form yourself again.

Release

Making Enabled was the best thing I ever did, just making it happen with Ceci was so much fun.

I think what the title Enabled means to me is that I'm able to accept myself as a person and to feel free. "Enabled" is so powerful, it means the opposite of disabled, not my favorite word. When you think of Enabled, think of freedom.

Release, cont.

I have always felt immense jealously for people
with exceptional memories of their childhood;
able to endlessly recall and recant vividly
detailed stories, conversations, people,
conflicts. I do not have this ability, much of my
memories are blurred together and fluid so that a
memory could come and go in an instant and if I
do not grab on to it, I will not be allowed it. I
much easier see blobs of color attached to past
time periods and feel parts of my body attached
to past emotions. I was initially angry at myself
for leaving behind scrolls and scrolls of crucial
evidence and research, but along this journey, I
realized that for me it is not important to know
exact conversations and details, because in my
memory I have found what I was seeking.
Redemption. Forgiveness. Connection.

My nineteenth birthday

This is her last month of being 18
Her last week
Can she do it?
Will she blossom into her future with little
time?
Is she ready to take a step of becoming a whole
new age?
She has now discovered she's an advocate for all
people who has learning challenges
She's learning about her learning challenge, but
wishes she didn't want it and being like her
friends
Normal, that's what she wants
She listened to her mom saying, "If you weren't
you, your dad and I will be so sad"
She spoke in front of legislators in Richmond
She managed to get a 4.0 GPA and A plus in a SDV
College class
She graduated from high school with her senior
class who were her friends
She has an incredible imagination and can write
beautifully
She's very, very good at being creative
She has inspired her own sister
Her dreams is to become the four different things
she sees herself do in the future
She wants to attend a four-year college
18 now becoming 19
Is this happening?
Feels like yesterday, she was born to perform in
the spotlight
Making everyone smile with hers
Light was her
She's light
Everywhere, even in the night.

Advice for people with Down Syndrome and their family members:

1. Inspire as many people you can
2. Be a team with your community
3. Advocate for yourself and become your own self-advocate
4. Share with the world you were meant to
5. speak up for yourself
6. Be informed
7. Stand up for inclusion
8. Band together
9. Don't lose hope

"No voice is too soft when that voice speak for others." -Janna Cachola

Dear sister, brother, parent, friend:

The birth of my sister is the best thing to ever happen to me.

The day she was born, I was almost three, and when my mom handed her to me wrapped in cloth, I believed my sister was a special gift from God himself to me. Today I am 22 and I feel the same exact way. There were many years where I didn't feel this way.

In those years I didn't understand how much I need her. Her and no one else. Because when I was formed, I was not complete. I was not complete until she was born because the person who was crafted of the same DNA as me was given a bit extra of what I was a bit deprived of. And vice versa.

Lucy and I don't like the word disability, because it is relative, and it is unfair to categorize her and not me (and not you) that way. What do you wish that you didn't have? For me it is anxiety, envy, an affinity to darkness, a restless heart. For you it might be a habit or a fixation or a health problem. For my sister it is Down Syndrome. We are all vulnerable to life, to ourselves.

You must remember that when you are close to someone, no matter who they are, it is your job to love them how they cannot love themselves. You must remind them, daily, of their worth, no matter how hard it can be to remember it. You must encourage, you must challenge, you must nurture them. You must not let them think they do not deserve the same opportunities as anyone else does. When they cannot hold themselves, you must hold them until they can.

Lucy has done this. All of this. For me. And I am not the one with the 'disability'.

I must try to do the same.

I hope that you know how lucky you are to have this role in someone's life. It is okay if you don't know how lucky you are already, but I hope I can remind you. You are lucky. Because then your capacity to love others will be greater and your capacity to love yourself will be greater. I guarantee it.

My sister and I climbed one of the highest mountains in the world together, us in all of our weaknesses and disabilities. There is no reason why we cannot climb higher.

Ceci Sturman

Dear person with Down Syndrome:

Nothing can stop you from your dreams. They are what make you strong, and you are too when have Down Syndrome. The inspiration of Down Syndrome inspires so many people in your life. Public speaking can helps you to speak with a voice that's very strong. It may be nerve-wrecking, but you were meant to be heard. You might be thinking, what does any of this means to me as a person with Down Syndrome? You're beautiful, special, and unique.

Well, like you, I have Down Syndrome. I was young and knew nothing about it until I was a teenager asking my parents questions, and of course, my doctor. I did some research and was very interested about what I was looking at. Throughout my life, my dreams kept me going and going and going, and they helped me to remind myself DS doesn't define who I am as a person. I'm advocating for you guys because I care about you and how God made you. You are a beautiful gift to the world.

You are an inspiration
To the world
The dreams, hopes, and hobbies
You have passion that helps you
To be the person you are
Together, you and me
Shows light in beautiful ways that other people can see
We were born to advocate for each other
We are more than Down Syndrome
We also God's gift of love and joy
No matter what
He loves all of us
Let's show the world who we are.

-Lucy Sturman

Footnote
Elizabeth Brookens-Sturman

The day Lucy was born was also the day we learned she has Down Syndrome; something we had no clue was coming.

Going in we were already worn thin. We'd been through 5 miscarriages and at 39, I was ready to give up. "Let's just accept it. Our family isn't going to be the way we've dreamed. Let's be happy with one child. Ceci is perfect."

John felt differently. As an only child, he's always wanted siblings so he wasn't ready to give our dream up. He was convinced we should try one more time.

In short, the news that Lucy was born with Down Syndrome knocked us both flat. We desperately needed help rising up from grief and disappointment that threatened to crush us.

First, we had to accept and understand 'Down Syndrome.'

Second, we needed to resist a very tempting and destructive narrative: "If only we had been satisfied with one child." Sadly, when you're sleep-deprived, thanks to a newborn's schedule and your own grief, it's easy to give in.

When I gave in it was ugly. I got angry at John for not listening to me. 'Ceci is perfect! An 'only child' would have been fine!' When John gave in he blamed himself for our pain and got depressed.

It wasn't that we didn't love and accept Lucy. We did and we do!

We just…didn't know.

We didn't know how capable Lucy could be. We didn't know that she would be hilarious and sassy and gregarious and sensitive and compassionate. That she would graduate with a 3.6 GPA; and place among the top half of her graduating class. That she would win high school talent shows with her dance routines. We didn't know that Lucy would be accepted into a highly competitive internship with the Virginia Board for People with Disabilities. That she would be selected to speak at advocacy events. That she could fully and independently maintain a daily routine. That she could write a memoir.

Looking back we realize God raised us up by surrounding us with SO MANY people. People who helped us see what we didn't see then. It's also what this memoir embodies.

Lucy is enabled; not disabled. And our lives. Our lives are more enabled because of her.

Looking back we can see that God surrounded Lucy and Ceci too.

You see, three years ago Lucy begged her dad and me to find a cure for Down Syndrome. With tears streaming down her face she told us she wanted to be 'normal.' 'Isn't there medicine I can take? There must be something!"

When we said 'there isn't a cure,' she said 'There's always prayer! Mom please pray and ask God to take it away.'

I took a big gulp. Eighteen years ago I did pray similar prayers. Not now. I told her if she didn't have Down Syndrome she wouldn't be Lucy. And if there isn't a Lucy that would make us sad.

It wasn't the outcome she wanted. She cried hard.

Yet, in her memoir it's clear. God surrounded her. God raised her up from her disappointment. Now Lucy is the one who helps others rise up when life doesn't turn out as they wish.

The same is true for Ceci.

You see, though we never intended this to happen, the subtle and not so subtle times John and I leaned into "Ceci is perfect" was a debilitating blow. At times our unrealistic expectations could knock Ceci flat.

Ceci tells us she felt we already had so much on our plates. Out of great love for us she didn't want to burden us more so she tried to battle her anxiety on her own. For eighteen years. There were many nights she didn't sleep; tossing and turning; doing her best to slay her fear. Then during the day she pushed herself to the brink to build her worth. All this; at great cost to herself.

It helps to know that even though we let Ceci down God didn't. Like God did for John and me and for Lucy~ God surrounded Ceci. God sent so many people along. People who helped Ceci find inner-peace and joy. Most powerful of all Lucy paved the way for Ceci's healing with her unrelenting and unconditional love.

In closing, the grief and disappointment that knocked John and me flat on the day Lucy was born is gone. Now we think of that day as the day that paved the way for all four of us to grow and heal.

Most important it's the day that set us on the path to discover what it means to be enabled!

I am so proud of Ceci and Lucy. I sincerely hope
that their memoir offers you hope. When life
doesn't turn out the way you want~ I truly
believe God will enable great gifts to rise out
of your grief and disappointment too.

Acknowledgments:

We are endlessly grateful to the **phenomenal, talented, giving, beautiful** people who have helped make this possible:

To Leslie Fernandez, Faith Vasko, Olivia Comm, Brittany Howard, Sheetal Dhir, Natasha Scripture.

To Jonathan Merlino, our photographer.
To Logan Koval for the cover design.

To Chief Editor Hannah Pruzinsky for immense support and for reading at least 25 versions of this.

Enabled

44078432R00093

Made in the USA
Middletown, DE
02 May 2019